your fres

AQUARIUM

a practical guide to setting up and maintaining a freshwater tank

your freshwater
AQUARIUM

a practical guide to setting up and
maintaining a freshwater tank

Maria Costantino

© 2011 Kerswell Farm Ltd

This edition published by King Books

Printed 2012

This book is distributed in the UK by
Parkham Books Ltd
Barns Farm, Boraston
Tenbury Wells
Worcestershire
WR15 8NB

david@kingbooks.co.uk

ISBN: 978-1-906239-83-1

DS0195. Practical Aquarium

Creative director: Sarah King
Designer: Jade Sienkiewicz
Project editor: Anna Southgate

Printed in Singapore

3 5 7 9 10 8 6 4 2

CONTENTS

in the wild

One of the most successful groups of animals on our planet, fish can be found in most bodies of water around the world, including seemingly inhospitable, sulphurous thermal springs and temporary, seasonal pools in the tropics that fill and dry up on an annual cycle. There are over 25,000 species in all. The vast majority of the world's freshwater fish live in warm water lakes and rivers, particularly in tropical Africa and America. Popular aquarium fish, such as tetras, angelfish and rasboras are among the brilliantly coloured, and differently shaped and sized fish that provide the aquarium keeper with such variety and interest.

Adapting for life

Whatever their habitat, fish are adapted to meet the demands of living and breeding there. For example, the upper reaches of tropical rivers are fast flowing and well oxygenated. The fish that live there need to be able to stand up to strong currents in order to find food. Such fish tend to have streamlined bodies, and, because the noise of water tumbling over boulders and the turbulence of the river flow make it hard to detect food by odour alone, these fish also rely on their eyesight for finding food.

As a river widens and slows downstream, currents become less strong and current-free pools often form along the course of the river. In this environment, a fish doesn't need to be so streamlined. Here species develop a deeper body shape, and, because the water is mostly clear, these fish identify and hunt their prey by sight.

Once a river reaches lowland plains, it widens out and the current slows. In tropical rivers at this stage the water is 'coloured' or clouded by organic debris and tannins that have leached into the river. The deep, darker waters allow little light to penetrate. The fish that live here have adapted to rely less on their vision and, instead, have better developed senses of smell and taste. Nearer the surface of this type of water, and at the margins, fish such as the tetras use their brilliantly coloured bodies to signal to one another and to keep to their shoals.

RIGHT: FISH BODY SHAPES AND SENSES HAVE ADAPTED OVER TIME TO SUIT THEIR HABITATS: THOSE THAT INHABIT FAST FLOWING STRETCHES OF RIVERS ARE MORE STREAMLINED; 'POOL' DWELLING FISH HAVE DEEPER BODIES, AND, IN 'MURKY' WATERS, THE FISH THERE RELY MORE ON THEIR SENSE OF SMELL AND TASTE THAN ON THEIR EYESIGHT.

your freshwater aquarium

LIFE IN PONDS

In contrast to tropical river environments are the habitats of tropical fish found in Southeast Asia. For much of the year, during the long, dry season, fish are effectively trapped in receding ditches and ponds of stagnant water that are choked with vegetation (which also shuts out the light) and so starved of oxygen. Nevertheless, the fish survive and thrive in these conditions, because they have adapted to them. Such fish are often small, as big-bodied fish would get tangled up in the thick vegetation. One of the most amazing feats of adaptation is the ability of some species such as the Anabantoids – the gouramis and their relatives – to breathe atmospheric oxygen using what is referred to as their labyrinth organ. This is located in the gill cavities and is constructed of a number of many-folded lamellae (thin sheets of tissue) that are rich in blood vessels.

When the rains arrive the ponds and ditches fill up and overflow across low-lying land and rice fields. The once shallow waters are now rich in food and the fish can grow and breed, but the water remains 'turbid' (opaque and muddied) and visibility may never exceed a few centimetres. Just as in the muddy waters of the Amazon, these fish must rely on their sense of smell and taste when it comes to finding food. Bottom-feeding fish have sensitive barbels – a bit like whiskers – on their lips that act like antennas to help locate food, while some gouramis use specially adapted pectoral fins to feel their way around their dark world.

LEFT: SOME SPECIES OF FISH SUCH AS THE ANABANTOIDS THAT INCLUDE GOURAMIS AND THEIR RELATIVES HAVE ADAPTED TO LIFE IN DITCHES AND PONDS OF STAGNANT WATER THAT ARE STARVED OF OXYGEN: THESE FISH BREATH ATMOSPHERIC OXYGEN USING THEIR LABYRINTH ORGAN LOCATED IN THEIR GILL CAVITIES.

Anatomy of a fish

Understanding the anatomy of a fish allows an aquarium keeper to understand how fish 'work'. This is the first step in ensuring that the environment created in an aquarium is best suited to the fish that will live in it. The shape of a fish's body gives clues as to its 'natural' life and habitat and, consequently, its needs when it is placed in an aquarium:

• Streamlined or 'torpedo' shaped fish are designed for open water swimming. They may also have a large caudal (tail) fin and a large tooth-filled mouth.
• Fish with tall 'laterally compressed' body shapes, like angelfish, inhabit slow-moving, reed-filled waters, so their bodies are designed to swim through plants.
• Vertically compressed body shapes belong to fish that live at the bottom of the water on lakebeds or riverbeds.

The position and direction of a fish's mouth – along with the presence or absence of barbels – indicates whether a fish is a top, middle or bottom feeder.

• An upturned mouth (with a bigger bottom lip) tells us that the fish feeds at the water's surface, approaching food floating on the surface from below. These fish usually have uncurved, straight dorsal (back) fins.
• Fish with a 'terminal mouth', where the 'snout' points straight in front of the head on a horizontal line along the body, are mid-water feeders. They approach their food head-on as it falls through the water (although they will take food from the surface and river/pond bed if they need to).
• Bottom-feeding fish have mouths that turn downwards so they can forage for food. Bottom-dwellers approach their food from above and use their sensitive barbels to locate the found particles buried in the substrates. These fish often have flat ventral (stomach) surfaces which help them lie against the riverbed. Many of the bottom-dwelling fish have whisker-like barbels around their mouths that are often equipped with taste buds so that a fish can forage and locate its food more easily.

ABOVE LEFT: 'TORPEDO' SHAPED FISH HAVE BODIES DESIGNED FOR SWIMMING IN OPEN WATERS WHILE 'LATERALLY COMPRESSED FISH' (ABOVE RIGHT) ARE ADAPTED TO LIVE IN DENSELY VEGETATED WATERS, THROUGH WHICH THEY CAN SWIM EASILY. FISH WITH 'VERTICALLY COMPRESSED' BODIES (BOTTOM) ARE ADAPTED TO LIVE ON THE FLOORS OF RIVERS AND LAKES. MANY OF THE 'BOTTOM DWELLERS' HAVE BARBELS OR 'WHISKERS' AROUND THEIR MOUTHS THAT THEY USE TO TASTE THE SEA OR RIVERBEDS FOR FOOD.

SCALES AND SCUTES

The scales on a fish not only provide protection, but also act as a streamlining device. A fish's body is covered in a slimy film of mucus, which acts as a barrier to keep out infections. The mucus on fish also contains protein compounds: the discus cichlid uses the mucus on its flanks to feed its fry, while other cichlids and some catfish actively 'dine out' on the protein-rich scales of other species by nipping them off with their teeth. Some scale-eating fish have even evolved colour patterns that mimic those of their prey, allowing them to swim among them before nibbling at them. A alternative to scales can be found in the armoured catfish group of fish: instead of scales their bodies are covered with two or three rows of overlapping bony scutes. While these protect the fish very well, they make the fish's body heavy and less flexible, so these fish are not such agile swimmers. To compensate for their lack of mobility and speed, these cumbersome armoured fish live happily at the bottom of the water on the riverbed.

FINS

Fish use their fins for locomotion and for stability and, in some instances, as aids in spawning during courtship or during the hatching period of eggs. There are two kinds of fish fin: single and paired, and they can be elongated and flamboyant structures that can be used to differentiate the sexes, although they are not always apparent on young fish.

Single fins

• The dorsal fin (on the back of a fish). The dorsal fin on a fish, such as the sailfin molly, may be erectile and will often consist of hard and soft rays.
• The adipose fin – if there is one – can be found on some species on its back near the tail. It is small and usually composed of fatty tissue: it's still not certain what the function of this fin is.
• The caudal (tail) fin. This gives the fish its final impetus to thrust through the water. But it's the S-shaped movements of the body that keeps a fish mobile. Fast-swimming fish generally have a deeply forked caudal fin.
• The anal fin is mounted on the underside of a fish's body, just forward of the caudal fin. This is mostly used as a stabiliser but in some species, like the male live-bearing fish, it has become adapted to be used as a gonopodium, a reproductive organ used for internal fertilisation of the female.

THE POSITION OF A FISH'S MOUTH IS ALSO INDICATIVE OF ITS FEEDING HABITS: UPTURNED MOUTHS (ABOVE) WHERE THE BOTTOM LIP PROTRUDES, INDICATES THE FISH FEEDS FROM THE SURFACE OF THE WATER, FEEDING OFF MORSELS FLOATING ON THE SURFACE. TERMINALLY POSITIONED MOUTHS (CENTRE) WHERE THE MOUTH IS IN THE MIDDLE OF THE FISH'S HEAD, INDICATE A MID-WATER FEEDER WHILE BOTTOM-FEEDING FISH (BELOW) HAVE MOUTHS THAT TURN DOWNWARDS AS THEY APPROACH THEIR FOOD FROM ABOVE.

Paired fins

• The pectoral fins emerge from just behind the operculum – the gill cover – and are primarily used for manoeuvring. Many aquarium fish have overlong, highly decorative pectoral fins that have been deliberately 'bred into' the fish. Such elaborate fin developments are not seen in the wild, where they would be highly impractical.

• The ventral fins (also known as pelvic fins) are situated forward of the anal fin. In fish like gouramis, these ventral fins are 'filamentous' and equipped with taste buds, which are used by the fish to help explore their surroundings. Angelfish, too, have narrow, elongated ventral fins but these aren't so manoeuvrable, while the armoured catfish use their ventral fins to transport their eggs to the spawning site. In some species of gobies, the ventral fins have become fused together to form a handy 'suction cup' that anchors the fish to the riverbed and stops it being washed away by the current.

Some fish may also have fin spines. These are used as protection against predators and can also be used by the fish to wedge themselves into safe, rocky nooks and crevices.

SWIM BLADDER

The hydrostatic buoyancy organ – known as the swim bladder – is exclusive to fish (although some fish, such as marine sharks, don't have one). The swim bladder allows the fish to position itself at any level in the water by automatically adjusting the fish to a 'neutral' density – that is, the same density as the water surrounding it. The deeper the water, the higher the pressure, so as the fish swims upwards through the water, the swim bladder alters the pressure inside the fish to balance it with its surroundings. Sport anglers of deep-water species, who 'catch and return' fish, have to reel in their catches slowly to allow the fish on the line to adjust to the changes in water pressure, otherwise the fish can die. In some fish species, the swim bladder also acts as an amplifier by picking up sound pressure waves as they pass through the water.

ABOVE: A VIEW OF A BOTTOM-FEEDING FISH'S BARBELS: THESE ARE SENSITIVE 'WHISKERS' THAT ARE USED TO TASTE AND TO PROBE THE RIVER OR SEABED FOR FOOD.
BELOW: A FISH'S SCALES PROVIDE PROTECTION AND ACT TO STREAMLINE THE FISH. THE SCALES ARE COVERED IN A PROTEIN-RICH 'SLIME' THAT ACTS A BARRIER TO INFECTIONS. FINS ARE USED TO PROVIDE BOTH STABILITY AND PROPULSION AND IN SOME FISH, ARE USED AS AIDS IN COURTSHIP AND SPAWNING. THERE ARE TWO KINDS OF FISH FINS: SINGLE AND PAIRED, BUT EITHER KIND CAN BE ELONGATED OR INDEED, VERY 'FLAMBOYANT' AND CAN BE USED TO DISTINGUISH BETWEEN THE SEXES.

your freshwater aquarium

COLOUR

Colour plays an important role in the wild, as it serves to identify the species of fish in general and the sex of fish in particular. Colour also provides fish with camouflage and can act as a clear visual warning that a species might be poisonous. The colour of a fish is determined by the reflection of light and by pigmentation. The silvery iridescent hues that can be seen on the flanks of many freshwater fish are the result of layers of reflective crystals of guanin, a waste product that is not excreted by the body, but instead is stored just beneath the fish's skin. The colour that is visible depends on the angle at which light hits and is reflected off the guanin crystals: you can see the colour changes for yourself when you observe a fish in an aquarium lit by light through the front of the glass tank and then look at the same fish from the top of the water with light coming directly overhead. Bright and well-defined colour and patterns on a fish in an aquarium are also an indicator of its well-being: when a fish looks dull, drab or 'washed out' compared to usual, it can be a sign to that it is ill or stressed.

Fish with deep colours have chromatophores – pigment cells – in their bodies and some species are able to control the amount of colour they display: you can see this most easily on fish species that like to rest on rocks or on the gravel bed of an aquarium where the fish's colours are adapted to suit their backgrounds. Other fish – such as the pencilfish – adopt nocturnal colours and each morning display a different colour pattern. Colour changes take place when the fish contract or expand the chromatophores to intensify or dilute the colour saturation in their bodies.

There are different types of chromatophores, each responsible for a different aspect of fish colour. One of the most important types of chromatophores is the melanophore: these contain the black pigment melanin and affect the darkness of, for example, the banding patterns on a fish. The melanophores are capable of responding very quickly to changes in a fish's mood or its environment. Other chromatophores contain different pigments and are responsible for different colours: the erythrophores hold the carotenoids (the same orange colour that is found in carrots), which affect the levels of red to yellow colours on a fish.

Young, immature fish will often be a different colour and have different colour patterns to older fish. Juvenile fish generally adopt quite drab colours: in the wild this would be sensible, as a brightly coloured young fish would be highly visible to prey fish and would not survive to adulthood. Once a fish reaches maturity though, it needs to attract a mate, and, consequently, a male fish's colour is likely to be heightened during the breeding period in order to attract a female mate. Some female fish in the cichlid group may also have a more intense colour so that their offspring can recognise their mother.

FISH COLOUR IS DETERMINED BY LIGHT BEING REFLECTED OFF ITS' SURFACE, BY LAYERS OF REFLECTIVE CRYSTALS THAT ARE STORED JUST BENEATH THE SKIN AND BY PIGMENTATION IN FOUND CHROMATOPHORES OR PIGMENT CELLS IN THEIR BODIES. THERE ARE MANY DIFFERENT TYPES OF THESE PIGMENT CELLS INCLUDING THOSE CONTAINING CAROTENOIDS THAT GIVE SOME FISH VIVID RED AND ORANGE COLORATION SUCH AS IN GOLDFISH (ABOVE) AND CELLS CONTAINING MELANIN, A BLACK PIGMENT THAT AFFECTS THE DARKNESS AND THE 'BANDING' PATTERNS ON A FISH, SUCH AS THE TETRA (BELOW).

FISH SENSES

Fish have the same five senses that we humans have: sight, touch, taste, smell and hearing. As mentioned, fish that inhabit clear water use their eyes in order to 'hunt'. Other fish, such as catfish, will use specially adapted parts such as whiskery barbels to 'feel' out their prey. The sense of touch is also enabled by the fish's lateral line.

Taste

Although they don't have a tongue like we do, many fish have an excellent sense of taste (known as gustation) and their taste buds are not just found in their mouths: the surface of many fish's bodies are covered in around 200,000 'extra-oral' taste buds, and many bottom-feeding fish – like catfish – have very sensitive taste buds in their barbels. As the fish swim along, they are 'tasting' for food.

Smell

Fish have a sense of smell. Some species of fish have two sets of nostrils: water is pumped in over one pair and out over the other pair so that the water passes over receptor cells that detect chemical messages. These are then decoded by the olfactory bulb located in the fish's forebrain. Fish use their sense of smell to navigate: each habitat has a unique chemical signature, and through experience fish become familiar with preferred areas in their habitat. The way fish move towards – or away – from a smell is called chemotaxis. Every animal produces its own distinct smell, so if a fish detects the smell of a prey fish on which it can feed, it follows the trace until the 'scent' becomes strong and it finds the source.

Hearing

Not so long ago, it was widely thought that fish were 'silent' creatures: they don't have external ears and, internally, they lack some basic structures for hearing. But in the early twentieth century, scientists conducted experiments that showed (and confirmed what many aquarium keepers long suspected) that fish could be 'trained' to emerge when a whistle was blown. Water is a very good medium for conducting sound: through water sound travels at about 1,500 m (1,640 yd) per second – faster than it does through the air – and fish use this to 'hear' and to communicate with each other. Sound travels through water as a series of vibrations and, because a fish's body is of a similar density to the water around it, the sound waves pass through it. However, in the fish's inner ear there are a series of tiny bones called otoliths that are of a different density to much of the rest of the fish's body. The sound waves cause these bones to vibrate, and it is these vibrations that are picked up by sensory cells in the inner ear and transmitted to the fish's brain. In some species, the swim bladder acts as an amplifier for sound waves, picking up on the pressure waves.

MOST FISH HAVE A SENSE OF TASTE- OR GUSTATION- ANY MANY OF THEIR **200,000** TASTE RECEPTORS ARE LOCATED NOT ONLY IN THEIR MOUTHS, BUT SPREAD OVER THE SURFACE OF THEIR BODIES. CATFISH BARBELS ARE EQUIPPED WITH MANY HIGHLY SENSITIVE TASTE BUDS SO THEY EFFECTIVELY 'TASTE AS THEY SWIM'.

your freshwater aquarium

Tip: Never tap on the glass of an aquarium! Because fish are extremely sensitive to underwater vibrations they can very easily be disturbed by high amplitude pressure sounds – such as those caused by tapping or banging on the glass of an aquarium. Continued disturbances such as this can severely stress the fish and lead to ill health and even death.

As well as hearing sounds, some fish also make sounds themselves: they don't have a voice box or vocal cords like humans but instead use two methods: stridulation, where the fish rub their teeth, spines or other bony skeletal parts together; and drumming, where the muscles around their swim bladders contract rapidly. The noises or 'songs' can range from the simple 'click' made by loaches to the more prolonged 'buzzing' and 'growling' sounds made by cichlids. The croaking gouramis, as their name suggests, make their sound by using their specially adapted pectoral fins. Most fish use the noises they make for courtship and to warn off any possible aggressors or threats to their territory.

Lateral line system and the sense of touch

Fish also have a sort of 'sixth sense' to help them 'hear' their environment and to find their way about in the water. This is known as the lateral line system: these are tiny perforations in a row of scales along both sides of the fish's body. The holes allow water to pass into the lateral line canal. This is lined with jelly-filled sacs that respond to changes in water pressure and changes in the flow or movement of the water. Many fish use their lateral line system to find their way about – especially in habitats where there is little or even no light for them to see by. The system allows the fish to 'map' their environment.

When a fish is placed in a new environment – such as an aquarium – it has to make a 'sensory map' of its new surroundings, and it does this by swimming quite fast and tilted to one side. This is to increase the flow of water over its body so the lateral line becomes extra perceptive and sensitive: it's a bit like when a human turns his or her head to listen to a faint sound. Sightless species of fish and nocturnal fish navigate and hunt prey in their environment by using their lateral lines to detect movements of invertebrates like shrimps: the vibrations caused by a passing shrimp are picked up by the lateral line and decoded by the fish, letting it know in which direction the shrimp is swimming – and enabling the fish to follow it.

FISH HAVE EXTREMELY SENSITIVE 'HEARING': NOISE TRAVELS AS VIBRATIONS THROUGH THE WATER THAT THE FISH SENSES USING ITS OTOLITHS, A SERIES OF TINY BONES IN THEIR INNER EARS AND IN SOME FISH, THEIR SWIM BLADDERS ACT AS AMPLIFIERS. CONTINUED AND LOUD DISTURBANCES- SUCH AS TAPING ON THE GLASS OF AQUARIA, OR TANKS POSITIONS TOO CLOSELY TO STEREO SPEAKERS- CAN CAUSE FISH T SUFFER AND DIE.

Fish behaviour

All life on Earth is governed by the 'rhythms of life'– the cycle of day and night and the changing of the seasons. During its lifetime, a fish has three main aims: to eat, to avoid being eaten itself and to reproduce. Fish behaviour is regulated by an internal biological clock that is synchronised to the cyclical changes in the environment by what are called zeitgebers, or 'time givers'. These zeitgebers are signals that act on a fish's biological clock, such as the arrival of dawn or dusk, or the rise or fall in temperature that indicates the arrival and departure of spring.

Most tropical fish species are diurnal – they are active during the day, when the light allows them to use their sight to hunt for food and avoid predators. In the tropics, day and night are about equal in length, so the fish are active for around 12 hours. However, it is in the first few hours that they are most actively seeking food to top up their levels of energy after a long night without food. In the wild, lake-dwelling fish move into shallow water, which is rich in invertebrate prey and once they have fed themselves, they move back to the relative safety of deeper water during the afternoon. Some fish, especially juveniles, may also move to 'warm spots' close to, or on the surface of shallow water where they bask: time spent in warm water speeds up the fish's metabolism and speeds up the conversion of their food in body growth. Growth is important, because bigger fish have fewer natural enemies, although basking does come with the associated risk of being swallowed up by a bird. But because birds are primarily visual hunters, they have to be actively seeking food during daylight hours and for the fish, the first sign that a bird might be too close for comfort is a large shadow cast on the surface of the water and the fish will swiftly dart to the relative safety of deeper water.

As day gives way to night, fish seek safe places to rest. Fish don't have eyelids, so they can't close their eyes and the closest they come to 'sleeping' is stopping moving and slowing down their breathing. Their lateral lines, which are able to detect movement in the water, keep a fish 'informed' of any predators in the vicinity and if one approaches, the fish will dart away with a flick of its caudal (tail) fin. Many diurnal fish also alter their colour during the night and adopt less visible colours: the pencilfish even changes its pattern from a horizontal band during the day to two or three vertical bands to help it blend in with the aquatic plants in which it shelters at night.

Not all fish can afford to rest though: in the wild, oxygen levels in the water drop and parental fish that are guarding their eggs or young often maintain vigil all through the night and use their fins to fan oxygenated water across the developing offspring.

MOST TROPICAL FISH SPECIES ARE DIURNAL- THEY ARE ACTIVE DURING THE DAY WHEN LIGHT LEVELS ENCOURAGE THEM TO FEED, MATE AND SPAWN. AT DUSK, FISH START TO SEEK SAFE RESTING PLACES: THE CLOSEST THEY COME TO SLEEPING IS BY SLOWING DOWN THEIR BREATHING AND KEEPING MOVEMENT TO A MINIMUM TO RESERVE ENERGY STORES UNTIL DAYLIGHT RETURNS. MANY DIURNAL FISH ALSO ALTER THEIR COLOUR AT THIS TIME TO MAKE THEM LESS VISIBLE TO NOCTURNAL PREDATORS.

FEEDING TIME

In the wild, fish synchronise their feeding activity with the availability of food and will often visit a particular feeding spot at a particular time of day, but generally will graze throughout the day on a variety of foods. In an aquarium, fish are dependent on having their food provided, but can still become accustomed to feeding at different times of the day in different parts of their aquarium. Many aquarium keepers will also notice that, when they add food to the tank, the fish go wild with excitement in a feeding frenzy. Their behaviour switches from a slow, calm and placid pace to fast and furious as they try to eat as much food as possible before it disappears into the mouths of their tank mates. This type of feeding behaviour also occurs in the wild when fish find a rich source of food and take their cue to feed from other fish already feeding. While in a tank the feeding fish may be safe from predators. In the wild, however, such frantic 'splashing' around can make the feeding fish a target for predatory fish and birds. In the wild there is uncertainty about when, or if, the next meal will be found, so it pays for a fish to gorge itself as much as it can. Fish have adapted to such a life by being able to expand their stomachs far mare than humans can in order to accommodate huge meals. And because fish store fat in a different way to humans, they don't get 'fat' like we do. As the food is broken down, digested and waste excreted, the fish's distended body reverts back to its 'normal' shape.

Just like humans, fish also have preferences in food and learn where these are, and how to catch them. Sometimes a change in diet is forced upon a fish if there is increased competition for the usual food. It is even possible for fish from the same species become morphotypes (members of the same species but with different appearances) and eat entirely different food.

Unlike humans, fish don't have hands to catch food, process it and carry it to their mouths! And unlike humans, who tend to chew their food one bite at a time, fish generally swallow up their prey in one gulp with very little chewing. One way that a fish feeds is to 'vacuum up' food: by opening its mouth and averting its jaw, a fish's buccal cavity is enlarged, which creates an area of low pressure and water rushes in from outside to equalise. Clever timing and gauging of distance can mean that prey is also 'sucked' into the fish's mouth. When a fish closes its mouth, the food is trapped within and the excess water is pushed out through the gills. Fish, particularly fish that eat other fish, have large mouths that allow them to create pretty powerful suction.

IN THE WILD, DIURNAL FISH ARE MOST ACTIVE IN THE FIRST HOURS OF DAY WHEN THEY MUST FEED AND REPLENISH THEIR ENERGY AFTER A LONG NIGHT. LAKE DWELLING FISH IN THE WILD WILL MOVE TO SHALLOW WATER AND, ONCE FED, RETURN TO THE SAFETY OF DEEPER WATER. IN AN AQUARIUM, DESIGNED TO REPLICATE THE FISH'S NATURAL HABITAT, FISH CAN NONETHELESS BECOME ACCUSTOMED TO FEEDING AT PARTICULAR TIMES OF DAY, AND WILL OFTEN RUSH TO THE FRONT OF THE TANK IN EXPECTATION OF FOOD.

TEETH

Teeth are an important part of a fish's anatomy and come in a wide variety of shapes, sizes and types, with each species' teeth adapted to its specialist diet. Many fish that are 'general eaters' – they'll eat whatever comes along – and have peg-like teeth that can grab and hold prey while the 'specialist' eaters, such as the sucking loaches, have flatter teeth that are designed for rasping at algae. Predatory fish have very sharp and backward-pointing teeth that trap struggling prey. Very often fish also have pharyngeal teeth situated in the roof of the mouth. Along with specialised tongues, the pharyngeal teeth offer extra grip on food. Freshwater habitats are home to a wide variety of shrimps, snails and molluscs and some fish species are adapted to deal with their hard, protective shells: puffer fish have bony beaks to bite open the shells to reveal the soft flesh beneath. Their beaks grow continuously and depend on a tough diet to wear them down. Some catfish and the clown loaches also enjoy snails and in these cases they are equipped with plate-like pharyngeal teeth and a powerful jaw muscles that 'crack open' the shells. Not all fish are 'carnivorous': the plec, the bristlenose and the whiptail catfishes are herbivorous and are well adapted to rasping off the rich algae film that falls on fallen wood or stones. Their mouths are located ventrally – beneath their flat bellies – and are powerful suckers that anchor the fish to the surface on which they are feeding. While the fleshy parts of their mouths hold them tight, their jaws rasp at the rock surface. Even their teeth are designed to accommodate the different types of algae: those that dine on soft algae have flat, broad teeth while for gouging on tougher substances, other fish herbivores have spoon-shaped teeth.

We might think its just dirt, but the bottom sediments of aquatic habitats are rich in decaying organic matter, from plant leaves and stems to the bodies of plankton and fish. This is home to numerous invertebrate animals that live or feed on the sediment and many fish species, known as 'detritivores', specialise in extracting food from it. There are also omnivorous species of fish, including the corydoras group of catfish and the geophagus cichlids (whose name means 'earth-eaters') that feed by sifting through the 'dirt' filtering out small particles of food.

Other species of fish also feed on algae but don't graze on it: instead they filter the algae out using their fine meshed gillrakers and secrete mucus to trap and collect the microscopic phytoplanktons. A few species, such as the silver dollar, eschew algae in favour of aquatic plants themselves: these fish have powerful jaws that bite pieces out of the plant, which can be a problem in the aquarium unless you install 'plastic' vegetation.

ABOVE: THE SILVER DOLLAR IS ONE FISH THAT HAS POWERFUL JAWS AND IS FOND OF BITING INTO VEGETATION PLANTED IN AQUARIA. MANY TROPICAL FISH KEEPERS OPT FOR PLASTIC PLANTS IN THIS SITUATION. BELOW: OTHER SPECIES FEED ON ALGAE: SOME SIFT THROUGH THE SEDIMENT USING THEIR BARBELS, WHILE OTHERS FILTER THE ALGAE USING THEIR FINELY MESHED GILLRAKERS.

your freshwater aquarium

Synchronised swimming

There's a slight difference between the two terms used to describe groups of fish: 'shoal' and 'school'. Marine biologists describe fish as schooling or 'in school' to indicate that the individual fish are a tightly knit 'unit', for example when they are all 'polarised' – that is, swimming or facing the same way. Shoaling describes less cohesive group behaviour but it is estimated that over half of the 25,000 known species of fish will shoal at some time or another. A shoal can consist of just two or three fish, or over a million, but whatever its size, the basic principles remain constant. Individual fish gravitate towards each other and are held in a 'community' by social attraction. When a shoal of fish is threatened, it breaks up and individual members scatter. Once the threat has gone, the individual fish use their senses of sight or seek out chemical clue traces in the water to find others and reform the shoal.

In the shoal, the fish have their own 'personal space' and maintain a distance between themselves and their nearest 'neighbour' with the distance between them related to the length of a fish's body. In normal circumstances, the fish are about two to three body lengths apart, but when they are hungry, the distances between fish can increase, and when threatened or swimming against a fast current, the distances between the fish can diminish so that the shoal 'tightens' into a ball shape as the fish on the outside and in most danger desperately try to get into the middle of the shoal.

Using their sensory skills the fish keep close tabs on their shoal mates: smell is important here especially if members of the shoal move out of sight. The sense of touch, via the lateral line, helps the fish to polarise and move coherently as a group. But it's a fish's eyesight that is vital in a shoal: many species signal to each other using their colour patterns on their fins and bodies. When a fish joins a shoal they join one that is made up of the same species as themselves, but it's also important that the fish in the shoal are of the same colour and similar size. Any fish that may be diseased or be carrying parasites is excluded from shoal membership: this is because for the shoal to operate effectively, all the individual fish must behave in the same way, must be able to swim at the required speeds, be able to live in the same habitat and eat the same kind of food. A shoal is like a beautifully matched corps de ballet, all dancing in time and in step to make a unified 'whole'. A fish that stands out from the shoal (perhaps because of its size) is like a solo performer, more obvious to a predator's eyes.

A SHOAL OF FISH (ABOVE) MAY CONSIST OF JUST TWO OR THREE FISH HELD TOGETHER IN A COMMUNITY BY SOCIAL ATTRACTION, BUT EACH FISH HAS ITS OWN PERSONAL SPACE. IF THREATENED, THE SHOAL WILL BREAK UP AND INDIVIDUAL MEMBERS DISPERSE, COMING BACK TOGETHER ONCE DANGER HAS PASSED. A SCHOOL (BELOW) IS WHEN THE FISH ARE IN A TIGHTLY KNIT UNIT SUCH AS WHEN THEY ARE POLARIZED- ALL FACING THE SAME WAY.

THE TRAFALGAR EFFECT

The Trafalgar Effect is the name given to the phenomenon by which an entire shoal of fish changes direction in the water. It takes its name from the way in which cannons were fired on the flagship at the famous battle, so giving the signal to the other ships in the line to start firing also. No matter how big or small the shoal, each fish has a relatively small number of near neighbours. The behaviour of nearby fishes exerts a strong influence on each individual fish to the extent that a fish copies what it's neighbour is doing.

When a shoal changes direction – when it meets and obstacle perhaps or senses imminent danger – the impetus always comes from a single fish (or a small number of fish) and those nearest the turning fish will replicate that movement. Those next to that fish will also turn, and so on through the shoal. To the naked eye, it often looks like the entire shoal is turning as though it was one fish, but on slowed-down video it's possible to see the 'wave' of activity passing through the shoal. Speed is still very important in the communication throughout the shoal, especially as it's important that a single fish doesn't 'stand out' from the crowd and become isolated, or it can become a predator's next meal.

Different species of fish use shoaling in different ways: some species, such as herrings are obligate shoalers: they must live in a social group and if isolated, they will die. Other species are facultative shoalers and use the advantages of community life when its suits them but will leave the shoal afterwards. Many species also shoal at certain periods in their life cycles: this is most common among fish when they are young and vulnerable to predators. Then, when they grow larger and older, they too may abandon the shoal to find their own territory.

Shoaling has both advantages and disadvantages for fish: living in a large group means competing for food and space, but on the plus side, the more eyes and noses looking for food, the better the chances of success, and, there can be safety in numbers if there is a predator around or when fish move into a new, unfamiliar environment. One benefit of being in a shoal is called 'attack dilution': most predators can only catch one prey at a time so a large shoal means the risk of being the 'chosen' individual fish caught in an attack are 'spread out' among the big number of fish in the shoal. Shoaling however is only effective against visual predators – those that hunt using their sense of sight – so at night, fish shoals tend to break up because concentrated shoals of fish would attract hunters who operate by smell to locate their prey.

The risks and rewards faced by fish in a shoal depend largely on its position in the group: in moving shoals, the fish at the front naturally get the first bite of food but they are also the first to come up against predators. In stationary shoals it's the fish at the edges that find the best food and face the greatest risk from predators. Fish do, however, change their positions in the shoal: when fish are hungry they swim faster and gradually move to the front of the shoal. Once they have found food and eaten it, they retreat towards the middle of the

THE TRAFALGAR EFFECT IS THE NAME GIVEN TO THE PHENOMENON WHEREBY AN ENTIRE SCHOOL
OF FISH CHANGES DIRECTION IN THE WATER BECAUSE OF AN OBSTACLE OR A THREAT.

your freshwater aquarium

shoal where they are safer from attack, and the hungry fish move forwards to take their place. Because fish in shoals rely on their neighbours, the species that do shoal are generally peaceful but fights can, and do, sometimes break out, particularly if the shoal has discovered a rich source of food. In such instances, it's every fish for itself and they will charge at each other, nipping and blocking access to the food for other fish.

Fish fisticuffs

Fish almost always fight over the same things: food, space and mates. They fight when these resources are in short supply, but how hard they fight depends on what's at stake: a fight over food will not be as intense as a fight for the attentions of a female fish. While some fish will fight to get as much food as they can, some species take this even further by staking out feeding territory and excluding rivals from their patch. Defending territory (and fighting for food) does, however, take up a lot of a fish's time and energy and so there must be a good 'payback': if the amount of food produced by the territory starts to decline, then defending the territory is not efficient and the fish will move on to a new place. Breeding territories with a good supply of food is a prerequisite for the many fish species that care for their young. For males hoping to attract a mate, the 'perfect' breeding territory is vital and, once found, this is vigorously defended against other males.

In the wild the largest and most dominant males get the best territories, because they are the strongest and most aggressive fighters. Dominance is generally acquired, first of all, by the fish fighting it out: fish newly introduced to each other will fight to see who is 'the boss' and continue fighting until an order of precedence has been established and calm returns. Some species, once the hierarchy has been established, produce a pheromone (from the Greek pherein meaning 'to carry'), a hormone that appears to promote peace and calm. When a fish is removed from one environment and placed in a new one- for example, moved from a pet shop aquarium to a new tank at home, where the fish have already worked out their hierarchy – the fish's behaviour in its new home will depend on its place in the hierarchy of its old home. If it was previously a dominant fish, then it will have to fight for a similar high rank; if it was at the bottom of the pecking order, then it will have to put up with the same situation in its new home.

FISH WILL FIGHT OVER TERRITORY, ESPECIALLY GOOD FEEDING, MATING AND SPAWNING GROUNDS IN THE WILD, THE STRONGEST AND FITTEST MALES ARE THE MOST AGGRESSIVE AND DOMINATE OTHER MALES WHILE IN THE TANK, DOMINANCE IS ALSO OFTEN FOUGHT FOR. ONCE A HIERARCHY HAS BEEN ESTABLISHED, CALM RETURNS.

The best breeding territories are bordered by less desirable spots – still good but not quite so good as the best ones – which are inhabited by the less dominant males and, in turn, these are surrounded by the least desirable spots with the weakest males. Nevertheless they are all defending their territories and not surprisingly, border disputes occur. When a female wants to mate with a dominant male in the prime location, the males in the neighbouring territories start displaying themselves frantically to try and persuade her not to leave. When two males meet each other on the borders of their adjoining territories, one fish adopts a threat posture and charges at his neighbour who, in turn, backs off. As the aggressor crosses the boundary into the neighbours' territory, he loses a little confidence and the retreating fish becomes emboldened and returns the charge. A lot of to-ing and fro-ing takes place with the boundary marked by a landmark – such as a stone or clump of weeds – but because each of the fish has to continue defending his territory from other neighbours, much of the time, a truce is declared with immediate neighbours. This stops petty squabbles with a few close neighbours escalating into all out war while allowing them to defend their space against 'alien interlopers' – real outsiders.

THE EGG-LAYING FISH SPECIES SPAWN IN DIFFERENT WAYS: THERE ARE EGG-SCATTERERS, EGG-BURIERS, EGG-DEPOSITORS, NEST BUILDERS, AND MOUTH-BROODING SPECIES. EACH SPECIES HAS ADOPTED A SPAWNING METHOD TO ENSURE THE SURVIVAL OF OPTIMUM NUMBERS OF OFFSPRING TO SUIT THEIR NATURAL HABITATS.

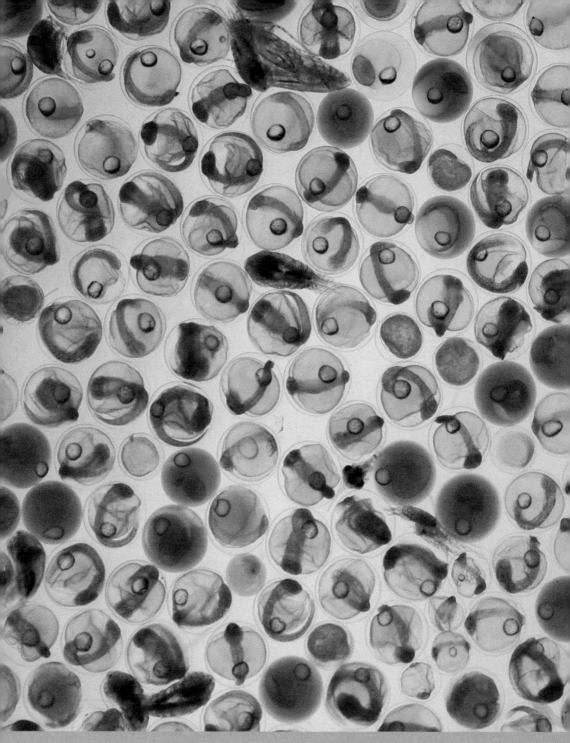

Breeding

Female fish are very particular about which male fish they choose to mate with and consequently, the males have developed a variety of 'courtship' strategies to attract females. The most obvious strategy is a male's bright colour, pattern and 'ornamentation' such as elongated fins, tails and bristles. Size also matters because it's only the strongest, healthiest and most able male fish that can forage for food and fight off rivals. A male's appearance is, therefore, an indicator to the female that he is a prime specimen, worthy of passing on his genes.

Once a female fish has made her choice of mate and they have successfully mated, the female will pass on her genes to her daughters. Encoded in the genes are the same ones that predisposed their mother to select a particular type of partner. Consequently, female fish offspring are genetically disposed to select mates that closely resemble their father, although some female fish, such as mollies, are known to imitate the choices of other female fish and consequently tend to mate with the most 'popular' male fish in the neighbourhood.

With females placing a great deal of emphasis on a male's 'display', you might wonder what happens to the less 'handsome' males who are scorned. For some species, this problem is resolved by forming 'pair bonds' where less 'desirable' males pair and mate with the less desirable females. Other species, such as guppies, have developed a 'hit and run' system: small and less brightly coloured male guppies are known rather appropriately as sneaks and use their speed and to sneak up on females and mate with them without any courtship ceremony. There are also some nest-making male fish who move next door to a larger male but adopt the colour and size of the females. These guys 'hang around' waiting for a real female fish to enter the dominant male's territory and spawn before dashing in and releasing their sperm over the eggs. The dominant male usually spots the 'transvestite' invader and chases him off, but it's often too late, as some of the eggs will already have been fertilised by him.

It's not only male fish that can be 'promiscuous': in order to ensure they get the strongest offspring possible, female livebearer fish will mate with any 'reasonable' male but after each mating, she becomes more and more fussy about her partner until she will only mate with the 'best of the bunch'. The female's promiscuity does have its benefits: if she held out for 'Mr Right' she runs the risk of not mating at all and procuring no offspring and, the multiple fathers of her brood ensure a diversity of genes that result in healthier fry.

THE SIAMESE FIGHTING FISH WAS FIRST BRED IN FRANCE FROM WILD STOCK IN 1893. DESPITE ITS NAME, THE SPECIES IS, IN FACT, COMMON TO MALAYSIA AND IT IS THE MALES OF THIS SPECIES THAT ARE AGGRESSIVE- BUT ONLY TO OTHER MALES. THIS IS WHY THESE FISH ARE BEST KEPT IN TANKS IN A MIXED TRIO- ONE MALE AND TWO FEMALES.

SPAWNING METHODS

The large majority of fish don't provide any care for their eggs or their offspring. The egg-laying fish spawn in a number of ways: egg-scattering; egg-burying; egg-depositing; nest-building or mouth-brooding. Egg-scattering fish release their eggs and sperm close together into the water column and let nature take care of the rest. This results in large numbers of fertilised eggs, but the adult fish are not in the least bit protective of them and, given the chance, they will eat them, but a tiny proportion at least survive to form the next generation of the species.

In flowing water, egg-scattering means that many of the eggs will get washed away by the current. To compensate for this danger, some species carefully place their eggs into a secure position either by burying them in the sediment on the river bed or by seeking out nooks and crannies in rocks in which to hide their eggs. Some species, like the harlequin rasboras, lay their eggs on the underside of broad-leaved aquatic plants. Species that 'place' their eggs have eggs that are necessarily sticky so they adhere to the plant or rock: because the eggs are in relatively safe environments, the female can afford to lay fewer of them. Nest-building fish collect fragments of plants to build nests to contain their eggs: the male Siamese fighting fish blows bubbles among the floating plants and debris to form a bubble nest. However, no matter how secure a nest might be, a certain proportion of the eggs – if not all of them – will be lost to predators. Some fish deal with this eventuality by carrying their young within them: the banjo catfish carries its offspring in hollows on the underside of their bodies while other species are mouth-brooders – they carry their brood in their mouths safe from predators (except of course, for those that prey on adult fish).

Mouth-brooding occurs in five freshwater fish species and across the range of species, there are both male and female mouth-brooders. The method ensures that more of the offspring are successfully hatched, but the number of fry is, in effect, limited to the size of the parent-carer's buccal cavity. Usually, the parent fish take the eggs into their mouths immediately after spawning and make gentle chewing motions to keep them nicely aerated. Even after they hatch, in many instances, the fry remain in the parent's mouths and are only released to feed. At the first sign of danger, the fry rush back to the safety of their parent's mouth. This effective method of rearing young is attractive to other species too: rather like in the bird world where the cuckoo lays its egg in another bird's nest, in the aquatic world, the cuckoo catfish swims among spawning cichlids and deposits its own eggs (often eating it's hosts eggs to make room for their own). The cichlids then gather in their eggs – along with the cuckoo catfish eggs – and carefully brood them as their own. Just like the cuckoo chick who tosses the 'true' eggs from the nest so they alone are the object of the parents' attention and care, once the cuckoo catfish hatch, they then feast on the cichlid eggs in the buccal cavity of their host.

GUPPIES ARE ONE OF THE MOST POPULAR TROPICAL FISH AND WERE DISCOVERED IN 1859 AND FIRST COLLECTED IN TRINIDAD IN 1866 BY DR. R GUPPY. A VERY HARDY LITTLE FISH, THE FEMALES PRODUCE ABOUT 100 YOUNG FRY EVERY 4 TO FIVE WEEKS- HENCE THEIR NICKNAME 'MILLIONS FISH'- AND THE YOUNG GROW VERY RAPIDLY.

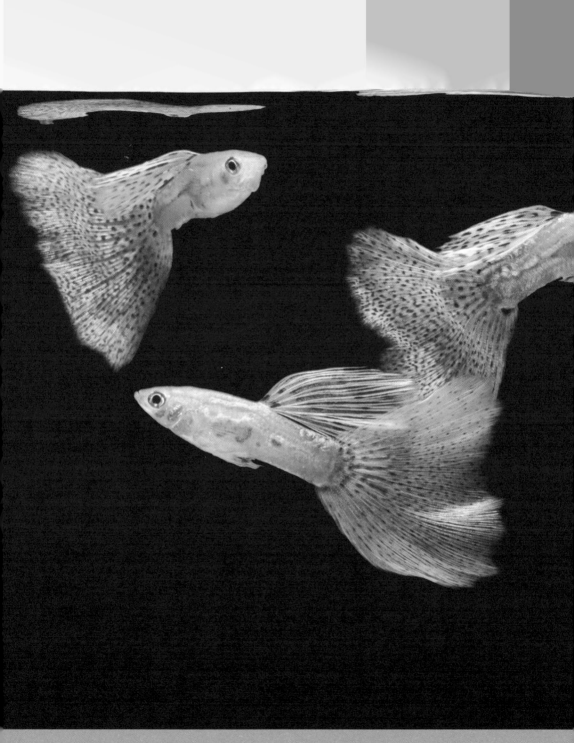

your freshwater aquarium

LIVE-BEARING FISH

Laying eggs works extremely well for the majority of the world's fish species and the odds of survival are balanced by some species laying thousands of eggs in the hope that a small proportion will survive, and others laying fewer eggs but caring for their offspring. Some species however, have adapted to skip the egg-laying stage completely and instead allow the eggs to hatch inside the mother's bodies where, during their first vulnerable days, they are safe.

The males of live-bearing species usually have specially adapted anal fins that are used to transport small quantities of sperm to the inside of the female fish. Once the eggs are fertilised and start to develop, embryonic fish such as guppies, platies and mollies feed on the yolk that is provided in the egg before fertilisation, while other species like the splitfin provide nourishment to the embryos from the mothers via structures called trophotaeniae, which are a little like the umbilical cords found in mammals. In most cases, once the embryos are developed and capable of independent life, the female gives birth as quickly as possible – usually one fry at time in quick succession.

ALL IN THE FAMILY

While each fish has to look out for itself, there remain strong bonds to the family. Using their senses – especially of sight and smell – the young offspring are able to identify not only their parents but also their siblings. In the wild, some parental livebearers won't cannibalise their own offspring, but will feast happily on unrelated fish, and some territorial species allow relations into their space to feed but fight off any unrelated trespassers. Some species, like the rainbowfish, form shoals of their relatives, while some cichlid offspring continue to remain 'at home' helping their own parents raise successive half-brothers and sisters.

THE GORGEOUS DISCUS WAS INTRODUCED TO THE AQUARIUM IN 1933 BUT IT WAS NOT UNTIL 1956 AND FOLLOWING INTENSIVE RESEARCH THAT BIOLOGISTS FULLY UNDERSTOOD THE REPRODUCTIVE HABITS OF THIS SPECIES. THE BREEDING PERIOD IS OCTOBER TO APRIL AND THE FIRST SIGNS ARE OF THE PAIR CLEANING A SUITABLE VERTICAL SURFACE FOLLOWED PERHAPS BY A LITTLE 'JAW LOCKING' IN COURTSHIP. THE SPAWNING OCCURS IN THE EARLY EVENING ON THE VERTICAL SURFACE- A PLANT OR THE WALLS OF THE AQUARIUM- AND THE EGGS HATCH IN FOUR DAYS. FOR THE NEXT THREE DAYS, THE PARENTS FAN AND CLEAN THE FRY UNTIL THEY ARE FREE SWIMMING. ONCE THIS OCCURS, THE FRY FEED DIRECTLY OFF THE PARENTS WHO EXUDE A FOODSTUFF THROUGH THEIR SCALES. WHEN ONE PARENT HAS BEEN PICKED CLEAN, HE OR SHE WILL DART AWAY, AND THE CLOUD OF FRY THEN CLUSTER AROUND THE OTHER PARENT TO FEED.

water: the essential element

Water: the fish's element

Understanding how fish live in their natural habitat helps the aquarist – the aquarium keeper – to recreate as accurately as possible the ideal conditions for tropical fish in a tank. With such a wide variety of fish to choose from it can be easy to be beguiled by their beautiful colours and fabulous fins, so it's important to remember that each species of fish comes from often vastly differing habitats in the wild, and, consequently, they will have completely different needs in an aquarium. The vital first step for the aquarist is to understand the complexities of the fish's natural element: water.

Water is 'simply' two parts hydrogen and one part oxygen, but, as we humans know, it looks and tastes different in different countries – and even in different parts of the same country. You can find out about the make-up of your drinking water from your water company. This is an important starting point: knowing the quality of the water that comes out of the tap will give the aquarist a clearer idea of what needs to be done to this water to make it suitable to support the fish.

RECREATING A BIOTOPE

Although water is the life support system for fish, in the tank it needs to closely replicate the type of water that a fish would thrive in naturally. Just as man has to recreate the Earth's environment for successful missions into space, the tropical fish keeper needs to recreate the fish's biotope – its original habitat. In the tropical aquarium key factors are conductivity levels, nitrogen levels, the pH levels (the level of acidity or alkalinity), the hardness or softness of the water, water temperature, mineral levels, oxygen and carbon dioxide levels in the water. In addition to the fish themselves, a biotope naturally contains plants, has light to stimulate both the fish and plant life, and elements that furnish the fish's landscape: gravel to replicate the lakebeds and riverbeds; rocks, roots and branches to provide shelter, territorial areas and even breeding sites.

THE AQUARIUM KEEPER IS RESPONSIBLE FOR RECREATING A BIOTROPE THAT IS AS CLOSE TO THE FISH'S NATURAL HABITAT AS POSSIBLE. THIS MEANS THAT THE WATER IN THE TANK MUST REPLICATE THE SAME LEVELS OF MINERALS, OXYGEN, NITROGEN AND CARBON DIOXIDE; THE SAME DEGREES OF ACIDITY OR ALKALINITY; THE SAME DEGREE OF SOFTNESS OR HARDNESS AND THE SAME TEMPERATURE IN WHICH THE FISH WOULD LIVE IN THE WILD. THE RANGE OF AVAILABLE TANKS (RIGHT) AND EQUIPMENT SUCH AS AN AIR STONE (LEFT) THAT 'FEEDS' OXYGEN INTO THE WATER IN A STREAM OF BUBBLES NOT ONLY ALLOWS FOR THIS REPLICATION, BUT ALSO OFFERS THE VIEWER AN AMAZING SPECTACLE OF SUBMARINE LIFE.

FRESHWATER pH COLOR CARD

6.0

6.4

7.0

7.2

7.6

TAP WATER: LETHAL FOR TROPICAL FISH

In water, ions conduct an electrical current from one point to another, and the level of conductivity is measured by the number of ions. In the Amazon River, the conductivity level is approximately 30 microSiemens (μS), but this does vary seasonally. Our tap water has a conductivity that varies between 400 and 1,200 microSiemens – a huge difference that has been caused by the addition of calcium, salts, metals, minerals and chemicals like chlorine gas and chloramine that make our tap water safe for us to drink. Other 'ingredients' in tap water include nitrates and phosphates – the levels of which will vary over the year – that leach into the watercourses from agricultural fertilisers that have run off fields. Putting tropical fish into a tank full of tap water is like sentencing them to death: to tropical fish, a tank full of tap water is a highly polluted environment. This means that the aquarist has to treat the tap water to make it safe. Even then, the water will only be suitable for certain species of fish.

CHLORINE AND CHLORAMINE

Chlorine gas is used for water purification. If it has been heavily used you will be able to smell it when you draw water from the tap. If you let the water stand for 24–48 hours, the chlorine gas will disperse naturally. You can speed up the process by agitating – stirring – the water or by placing an air stone in the container with the water. A dechlorinating agent can also be used: these are available in liquid form from aquatic stores and are mixed into the aquarium water in the proportions given on the label.

Chloramine is another chemical added to tap water by some water companies. It does not disperse naturally, so if it has been used in your water area, the aquarium water will need to be neutralised with a water conditioner (which, incidentally, will also deal with chlorine). You can ask your water company if they use chloramines (and any other chemicals) and many water companies will inform aquarists if they are going to flush the water mains to kill any 'bugs' that may also affect the health of fish.

Did You Know? Water drawn though copper piping can be toxic to fish, especially if the pipework or water storage tank is newly installed. The first batch of water drawn from the tap has usually been standing in the pipes or tank for some time and should not be used for the aquarium.

THE ACID TEST: A pH TESTING KIT IS VITAL AS THIS ALLOWS THE AQUARIST TO ACCURATELY MONITOR (AND THEREFORE ADJUST) THE ACIDITY OR ALKALINITY OF THE WATER IN THE TANK. THIS TEST IS CARRIED OUT DURING THE PREPARATION OF THE WATER AND THE TANK, READY TO RECEIVE THE FISH, AND IS REPEATED AT REGULAR INTERVALS DURING TANK MAINTENANCE TO ENSURE A 'HEALTHY' WATER.

Tip: Some specialist aquarium shops will test your tap water for you to see if you can use it in an aquarium. You can also buy osmosis water – normal tap water that has already been filtered – and demineralised water – all the minerals have been taken out.

Tip: If you have access to tap water only, remember that your choice of animals and plants in your aquarium will be limited to those that can live in this habitat.

Tip: If you shop locally for your aquarium stock, the fish and plants stocked by a local dealer will have been kept in water very similar to your own while they await sale. If you buy more exotic species that require specialised water conditions, or are buying fish from outside your local area, ask the supplier about their local water conditions to see if they vary significantly from your own.

Warning: NEVER use collected rainwater in an aquarium. While it might seem purer than tap water, rainwater doesn't contain any of the essential minerals vital for maintaining stable water conditions. Rainwater can also contain pollutants picked up from the atmosphere after dry spells – and it may even contain poisonous leaves or the bodies of dead insects picked up from the guttering.

THE PH VALUE OF WATER

The pH scale measures the strength of acidity or alkalinity in water on a range from 0 (very acid) to 14 (very alkaline) – pH 7 is the neutral point, neither acid nor alkaline. The scale is logarithmic: this means that, for example, a measure of pH8 is ten times more alkaline than pH7, and a pH9 is one hundred times more alkaline than pH7. For the aquarist, the pH scale is important because only a narrow 'band' of water between pH 6.5 and pH 8.2 is suitable for freshwater tanks. In most European domestic water supplies the pH of tap water is around 7.2, whereas in the USA, the pH level of tap water is around 7.8–8.2.

The pH levels of water in the tank are important because freshwater fish from jungle streams and rivers are generally found in waters with a pH level below 7, whereas fish from the rocky basins need water with a high mineral content and a pH of higher than 7. In a 'cosmopolitan' community of varied tropical fish, slight variations in pH levels are not generally a problem but attention must be paid to the types

THE RELATIVE HARDNESS OR SOFTNESS OF WATER IS DUE TO THE AMOUNT OF MINERAL SALTS- USUALLY CALCIUM AND MAGNESIUM- DISSOLVED IN IT. BOTH MINERALS ARE VITAL FISH AND PLANT NUTRIENTS AND WHILE MOST SPECIES OF EGG LAYING FISH PREFER SOFTER WATER, SOME PLANTS AND LIVE BEARING FISH (AND CICHLIDS OF AFRICAN ORIGIN) PREFER HARD WATER. SPECIALLY DESIGNED AQUARIUM WATER SOFTENERS CAN BE USED TO REDUCE LEVELS OF HARDNESS.

API®

Aquarium Pharmaceuticals

WATER SOFTENER PILLOW

FILTRATION MEDIA TO REDUCE GENERAL HARDNESS

SOFTENS HARD WATER

REMOVES CALCIUM & MAGNESIUM

Ca^{2+}

Mg^{2+}

CHEMICAL FILTRATION

3 BIOLOGICAL

2 CHEMICAL

MECHANICAL

SCIENTIFICALLY PROVEN - REDUCES GH

EN Softens hard aquarium water
Ready to use pouch
For fresh water

Adoucit l'eau calcaire d'aquarium

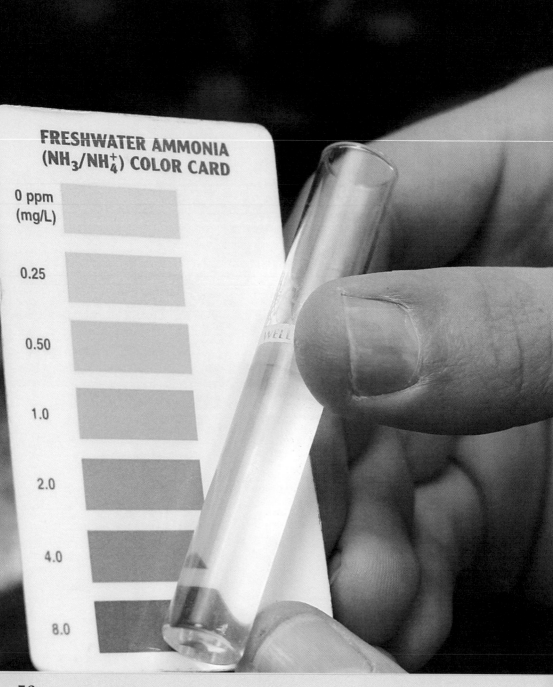

FRESHWATER AMMONIA
(NH_3/NH_4^+) COLOR CARD

0 ppm
(mg/L)

0.25

0.50

1.0

2.0

4.0

8.0

your freshwater aquarium

of gravel and rocks that are added to the tank, as these can alter the pH levels. Sometimes, too, the more experienced aquarist will want to stabilise the pH at a particular level – to encourage breeding for example – or to maintain a highly specialised colony of fish in the aquarium.

The pH of any water sample can be easily tested using an inexpensive water testing kit: a sample is taken and a liquid indicator is added and the mixture's colour is then compared with those on a calibrated colour wheel and the pH value of the sample can be read off against the scale.

WATER HARDNESS AND SOFTNESS

The hardness of water is another significant factor in the well-being of fish in an aquarium. The relative hardness – or softness – of water is due to the amount of dissolved salts – usually calcium and magnesium – in the water. The hardness or softness of the water that is supplied domestically by water companies will depend on its source or place of origin: water pumped from mountainous reservoirs is generally soft, whereas water collected from chalk soils is generally hard.

Calcium and magnesium are important nutrients for plants and animals and are important for the skeletal development of fish. There are two types of hardness: general hardness (Gh) and temporary or carbonate hardness (Kh). Temporary hardness (Kh) can be removed from water by boiling it but general hardness (Gh) can only be removed by distillation or by chemical means using special aquarium water softeners. Most species of egg-laying fish prefer soft water environments because any excessive hardness in the water can prevent the development of fertilised eggs. Live-bearing fish and some of the cichlids of African origin need a hard water environment. The same preferences are true for the different plants – and other underwater life – that will also live in the aquarium biotope.

In the aquarium, hardness is the amount of calcium carbonate ($CaCO_3$) and is measured in degrees of hardness (odH) or in parts per million (ppm). Buy a test kit for water hardness and then choose your fish to suit. You can tell if the Gh value of the aquarium water is wrong by looking at the shells of water snails: if their shells are white they are suffering from a calcium deficiency. In relation to the pH levels (see above), hard water is usually alkaline (above the neutral pH7 mark), while soft water is generally more acidic (below the pH7 neutral mark).

AMMONIA IS EXCRETED BY FISH THROUGH THEIR GILLS AND WASTE PRODUCTS AND IS ALSO PRODUCED BY DECOMPOSITION OF UNEATEN FOOD AND DECAYING VEGETATION. IN THE WILD, THIS AMMONIA IS BROKEN DOWN IN THE NITROGEN CYCLE BY BACTERIA INTO NITRITES AND THEN INTO NITRATES (A FORM THAT CAN BE ABSORBED BY PLANTS). IN THE TANK, THE LEVELS OF AMMONIA (IN THE FORM OF NITRITES AND NITRATES) MUST BE MONITORED CAREFULLY AND KEPT IN CHECK BY BENEFICIAL BACTERIA LIVING IN THE AQUARIUM'S FILTRATION UNIT.

IRON FOR VITALITY

Just as we humans need iron in our diets, so do plants. When humans have an iron deficiency, they suffer from anaemia, a reduced number of red blood cells, which are vital for circulating oxygen around our bodies. Anaemia causes us to become tired, weak and breathless but we can bring our iron levels back to normal by taking an iron pill or supplement. Plants also need iron – in miniscule amounts – to help maintain their green or red colours: plants in the aquarium that are turning yellowish indicate an iron deficiency and so iron must be added to bring the levels back to normal. This needs to be done on a daily basis (you can get iron for the aquarium at pet shops) because the tiny amount of iron degrades – it rusts – due to the presence of oxygen in the water. Once the iron has disintegrated it cannot be absorbed by the plants. Remember that the plants in the aquarium are part of the biotope you are creating: healthy plants are vital for healthy fish.

OXYGEN AND CARBON DIOXIDE

An aquarium needs the right number of plants to maintain the oxygen and carbon dioxide levels. Plants 'inhale' carbon dioxide during daylight hours and at night they 'exhale' oxygen, so the amount of time an aquarium is lit up to simulate daytime is crucial. If the aquarium is lit for 20 hours a day, the plants will only will have only four hours to make the oxygen that is vital for their life – and that of the fish in the tank. If time is too short to produce oxygen, the plants will, along with the fish, wither and die. Like a human being, no fish or plant can survive without oxygen: in an aquarium, the size of the tank, the number of fish and the number of plants need to be in balance so the oxygen levels remain constant for healthy life.

BACTERIA: GOOD AND BAD 'BUGS'

If you notice fish coming often to the surface of the water to breathe, then there is something wrong: the water is not oxygenated enough and the surface of the water needs to be moved with an air pump so that the oxygen can be absorbed. You also need to find the reason for the oxygen deficiency: there might be too many plants or too many fish for the size of the tank; the length of 'daylight' might be too long and the plants don't have enough time to restock the oxygen levels; or there might be too many bacteria in the tank, they can soon create an oxygen-deficient environment.

BECAUSE THE AQUARIUM IS EFFECTIVELY A 'SEALED' AND 'ARTIFICIAL' WORLD, THE PLANTS AND FISH THAT LIVE WITHIN IT MUST BE SUPPORTED: PLANTS REQUIRE FEEDING (TOP LEFT) AND OXYGEN MUST BE PROVIDED (TOP RIGHT) IN ORDER THAT HEALTHY LIFE IS SUSTAINED (BELOW).

your freshwater aquarium

Bacteria are vital for ensuring that the fish and plant waste products are converted in nutrients. The most important bacteria in the aquarium are Nitrosomonas bacteria in the biological filter (and coating the surfaces of the aquarium) that convert ammonia to nitrite, and Nitrobacter and Nitrospira bacteria that convert the nitrites to less harmful nitrates, that can be used by plants as fertiliser. As they undertake this vital process, the bacteria use a great deal of oxygen and if there are too many bacteria in the tank, they can soon create an oxygen deficient environment.

THE NITROGEN CYCLE

One of the most important chemical processes to take place in the aquarium is the circulation of nitrogen-containing compounds, known commonly as the nitrogen cycle. This is the natural process by which dead and decaying waste material that contains nitrogen is converted by bacteria from poisonous chemical compounds, like ammonia (which is excreted by fish through their gills and their waste products), into more harmless substances, such as nitrates, that are used by plants in their growth. The cycle begins as soon as a tank is set up and the filtration system is running. Once the filtration system is colonised by beneficial bacteria, it becomes more efficient. But as soon as you add fish to the tank, the system becomes overloaded. It takes a few days for the bacteria to grow in sufficient numbers to cope with the extra fish waste. For this reason, aquarists add fish one or two at a time to the aquarium – not all at once – so the bacteria can increase and the fish don't get upset.

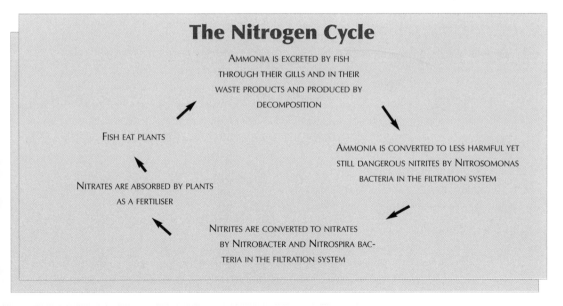

The Nitrogen Cycle

AMMONIA IS EXCRETED BY FISH THROUGH THEIR GILLS AND IN THEIR WASTE PRODUCTS AND PRODUCED BY DECOMPOSITION

FISH EAT PLANTS

AMMONIA IS CONVERTED TO LESS HARMFUL YET STILL DANGEROUS NITRITES BY NITROSOMONAS BACTERIA IN THE FILTRATION SYSTEM

NITRATES ARE ABSORBED BY PLANTS AS A FERTILISER

NITRITES ARE CONVERTED TO NITRATES BY NITROBACTER AND NITROSPIRA BACTERIA IN THE FILTRATION SYSTEM

ONE OF THE VITAL PIECES OF TANK EQUIPMENT IS THE FILTRATION UNIT: THIS IS COLONISED BY BENEFICIAL BACTERIA THAT HELP KEEP HARMFUL LEVELS OF NITRITES AND NITRATES TO A MINIMUM.

REGULAR WATER TESTING IS ESSENTIAL

In a perfect circle, the plants would take up all of the nitrates as fertiliser, but in an aquarium there is often too much waste for the plants to use, and the result is dangerously high nitrate levels. The only way to remove these is to carry out regular, partial water changes. In addition to reducing the nitrate levels, changing some of the water in the aquarium also replaces any lost nutrients and minerals that keep the water condition – and that of the aquatic life – stable. The amount of water that is changed depends on the level of the nitrates, so regular water testing is essential.

Tip: In general, changing 10–20% of the water every two weeks keeps the conditions stable. Remember to take water from the coldwater tap, treat it with a dechlorinator and leave it to warm up to room temperature before using it.

Temperature

Tropical fish, as their name tells us, are native to warm tropical waters. Consequently, for these fish to be happy in an aquarium, the water temperature must resemble that of their natural habitat. The waters that tropical fish – and the plants that they live among – are found in are a balmy 23–26°C (73–78°F) and the water in the aquarium must be the same. Outside of this range – too warm or too cold – their bodies cease to function properly and they die. It's important to remember, however, that the temperature of water also affects its oxygen content: the warmer the water, the less oxygen it holds. Any fish species that are unaccustomed to the warmth will often been seen gasping for air at the water's surface. In cooler conditions, the fish will slow down and lie close to the bottom of the aquarium. Plants, too, will struggle with what, to them, is intense heat or arctic chill: too warm and they might grow too big and straggly before collapsing with exhaustion; too cold and they'll shiver and won't grow at all. Just as in our homes, this means that aquariums need a heating unit, a thermometer, and a thermostat to keep the water temperature constant.

BEFORE ANY FISH CAN BE INTRODUCED TO THE AQUARIUM, THE CONDITIONS IN THE TANK MUST BE 'PERFECT': THIS INCLUDES NOT ONLY THE WATER QUALITY, BUT THE WATER QUANTITY, ITS TEMPERATURE, AND ITS AERATION. THE FILTER NEEDS TO BE WELL COLONISED WITH BACTERIA TO BE ABLE TO DEAL WITH THE AMONIA EXCRETED BY THE FIRST FISH TO ARRIVE IN THEIR NEW HOME (ABOVE). DURING ROUTINE 'HOUSEKEEPING' THE TANK KEEPER WILL BE MONITORING THE WATER QUALITY AND REPLACING A PROPORTION OF THE TANK'S WATER WITH 'NEW' PREPARED WATER THAT IS ADDED GENTLY SO IT DOESN'T CAUSE A 'TIDAL WAVE' IN THE TANK (BELOW).

your freshwater aquarium

Water, water, everywhere

Understanding a little about the water chemistry helps to recreate a 'natural' environment that tropical freshwater fish will thrive in. Nevertheless, there is still some way to go to creating the perfect biotope: the fish need the 'human equivalent' of a house, and, just as there are tall, short, fat, and thin people, living spaces for fish need to be of the appropriate size! And a house isn't a home until it's furnished: just as floors need carpets, an aquarium needs a substrate to replicate the riverbed or lakebed. It also needs plants for food (and oxygen), swimming, resting and hiding between and 'rooms' – territories that each species or individual can call its own.

The following section shows how to choose an aquarium, how to ensure you have the right equipment, and how to furnish and decorate it to make it the ideal home that its fishy inhabitants will enjoy living in.

TOP: MANY OF THE 'IN TANK' PIECES OF EQUIPMENT SUCH AS FILTERS AND HEATERSTATS ARE DISGUISED BY PLANTING OR TANK FURNISHINGS. ONE ESSENTIAL PIECE OF KIT IS A THERMOMETER AS THE TEMPERATURE OF THE WATER MUST BE TAKEN TWICE DAILY. THERMOMETERS CAN BE 'IN TANK' (ABOVE) AND ATTACHED BY SUCTION TO THE FRONT PANEL OF THE TANK SO IT CAN BE EASILY READ. THERE ARE ALSO 'STICK ON' DIGITAL THERMOMETERS THAT CAN BE ATTACHED TO THE OUTSIDE, BUT WHICH EVER YOU CHOSE, IT SHOULD HAVE MARKINGS THAT ARE CLEARLY VISIBLE, AND IDEALLY SCALED IN BOTH FARENHEIT AND CENTIGRADE (BELOW) FOR EASY CONVERSION.

selecting and setting up an aquarium

Once established, tropical aquarium fish are relatively inexpensive to maintain and their beautiful appearances and intriguing behaviour will give many hours of pleasure, but before you begin, you need to plan for the necessary aquarium equipment, its furnishings and of course, its inhabitants.

Time is important

Setting up a freshwater aquarium to create a suitable habitat for fish doesn't happen overnight: before you buy your fish, you need to prepare for their arrival. Furthermore, we've already seen how the water quality is vital to sustaining healthy life and the aquarium water needs time to stabilise before any fish are introduced. It's also important to remember that the size of the aquarium dictates both the volume of water it can hold (which contributes to the overall weight of the tank) and the size and number of fish that can live happily in it.

DON'T BE AFRAID TO ASK

For the novice aquarist the amount of information, skill and knowledge required to set up and maintain a healthy aquarium may seem daunting but, as with all specialist interests, help is at hand. Clubs are a great way of sharing information and skills and membership of an aquarist club is invaluable in providing a network of well-informed people who are only too willing to share their skills and advice. Aquarist clubs are also a good way for novices to find out which suppliers of fish (and accessories) have the best reputation for providing healthy fish and all that is needed to keep them in peak condition, so be guided by people with practical experience. Club members, too, will be happy to help you set up your tank and equipment, and may even have one or two bits and pieces that they will give you to get you started.

SPECIALIST AQUARIUM SUPPLIERS

General pet stores will no doubt have tropical fish and tanks in their stock and they may have staff who are enthusiasts and keepers themselves. A specialist aquarium supplier however, is more likely to have a wider range and be able to provide useful guidance on buying and stocking a tank. A good aquatic dealer will understand that everyone has to start somewhere – and will realise that the novice tropical fish aquarist is a long term customer in the making, so it's worth their while to spend time and energy with a newcomer. The best time to shop is on a quiet day in the week, perhaps first thing in the morning: this means the owner will be able to spend time with you. On busy weekends, a reputable supplier might ask you to return on another day so time can be spent advising on your particular needs.

THE RANGE OF EQUIPMENT AVAILABLE CAN BE QUITE BEWILDERING FOR THE NOVICE- NOT TO SAY EXPENSIVE. MAKE SURE YOU GET THE RIGHT EQUIPMENT THAT IS SUITED BOTH FOR THE TYPE OF FISH YOU INTEND TO KEEP AND TO YOUR HOME.

your freshwater aquarium

LOCATION, LOCATION, LOCATION

The first consideration is where in your home you will site your aquarium. The size of space available in a room will impact inevitably on the size of aquarium but there are also some other important factors to consider. The tank will need to be sited close to power sockets otherwise you'll have yards of unsightly power cords trailing around the room that are not only unsightly but can be dangerous trip hazards. Remember, too, that water and electricity are a potentially lethal combination: cables should be positioned with a 'drip loop' – where the cables hang below the socket so that any water that may run down the cable doesn't drip into the socket.

Weight is another factor to consider: 1 litre (2.1 pints) of water weighs 1 kg (2.2 lbs); 1 gallon (8 pints) weighs about 10 lbs (4.5 kg). A tank measuring 60x30x38 cm (24x12x15 in) holds 15 gallons or 68 litres and the water alone will weigh 68 kg (150 lbs). Now factor in the weight of the tank itself, the cabinet or stand on which it will sit. Add on the equipment, the substrate (gravel bed) and any rocks and you've got one very heavy piece of kit!

Don't even think about placing a tank – even a small one – on book shelves (or even coffee or side tables) because, unless they have been designed to bear heavy loads, you could be looking at a disaster. Consequently, the floor on which the tank sits must be strong enough to take the combined weight. If you have a concrete floor, there's no problem, but if you have wooden floorboards, then look for a site where the tank and base can sit on and be supported by the joists rather than the floor boards themselves (which may bend and warp under the weight). To find the joists, look at the direction of the floor boards: the joists generally run at 90° to them and you will be able to see where the joists are by looking for where the floor boards are nailed or screwed down into them. If the room is carpeted do expect that the weight of the tank will 'crush' the pile and don't forget that when the tank is full of water and fish, it will be extremely difficult to move it, so decide on your ideal location before filling it up!

GOOD – AND BAD – POSITIONS

While you will want to sit comfortably and view the aquarium from the comfort of your favourite armchair, some locations in a room are more suited than others for siting the tank. Remember that the aquarium is a substitute biotope and the 'happiness' of the fish is paramount, so be prepared to move your chair to a different spot in the room!

In the end, the final position of the tank is really a matter of compromise but some sites are still better than others – for both the fish and the owner. Good sites for tanks are in quiet corners – often the dark

THE LOCATION OF A TANK IS IMPORTANT AND YOU NEED TO TAKE INTO ACCOUNT A NUMBER OF FACTORS INCLUDING SPACE, SAFETY, STABILITY, AND SERENITY- FOR BOTH YOU AND THE FISH.

or 'dead space' in a room – and these can be enhanced by the addition of an attractive aquarium. The corner should be far enough away from doors so that draughts and vibrations caused by doors closing (or slamming shut) do not adversely affect the fish. Siting the tank away from doors also means that the fish aren't disturbed by passing human 'traffic', and because they are acutely sensitive to vibrations, make sure the tank is well away from stereo speakers, televisions and other domestic items: a kitchen is not the place for an aquarium as there's too much human and electrical activity and cooking fumes may also affect the health and well being of the fish. Alcoves are often ideal spaces to locate a tank – provided they allow you room to access the tank for servicing and cleaning and are close to a power supply.

Don't site your tank next to a central heating radiator (or fireplace) or where it will be in direct sunlight: this will not only raise the water temperature, it will also stimulate the growth of unsightly algae. Draughts, too, from windows and open fireplaces can lower the temperature of the water so avoid placing the tank close to these features. With regards to light, you may want to consider fitting dimmer switches to the room lights: these will help reduce the shock to the fish of sudden changes in darkness and light. Note, however, that dimmer switches do produce an audible 'buzzing', so make sure the tank is not situated under or next to the dimmer switch itself.

Choosing a tank

Selecting a tank is a lot like choosing a home: it has to be big enough to accommodate the inhabitants – and any offspring that might come along and it needs to be in the right location. Furthermore, the aquarist has to live with the tank in their home so the design and style should be pleasing to the owner too. A tank – and its necessary equipment such as heater, lights and filtration system – all need to function well and continuously with minimum maintenance.

Before you buy your tank, take a few measurements of the room and draw a floor plan to work out the location: this will also help you visualise the 'right size' of tank for the room – and make sure that it will fit through your doors!

TANKS COME IN VARIOUS SHAPES AND SIZES, EACH SUITABLE TO AN OP-
TIMUM SIZE AND NUMBER OF FISH: TOO SMALL A TANK AND THE FISH
MAY SOON OUTGROW IT AND SOME FISH PREFER TO LIVE IN SOCIAL
GROUPS SO NEED ROOM TO SWIM FREELY.

your freshwater aquarium

It's also a good idea to consider any humans – especially children – who share your home. Children are inevitably fascinated by the wonderful colours of tropical fish, so it's a good idea to position a tanks where they can be viewed safely and where children won't 'bang into them' – or indeed, tap on the glass (the vibrations upset the fish). Raising the tank above the height of small children is a good idea: the last thing the fish will need is an extra portion of fish food offered lovingly by a child!

SIZE MATTERS

As mentioned earlier, the bigger the tank, the more stable the conditions for the fish and the easier it is for the keeper to maintain. Large tanks give fish more room in which to swim and set up viable territories but more importantly the larger the surface area of the water, the better the supply of oxygen and exchange of gasses: a tall, narrow tank may hold the same volume of water as a long, shallow tank, but the latter is better for ensuring the vital supply of air.

Below is a table to give an idea of the sizes, volumes and weight of water for a range of standard tanks:

Tank dimensions	Volume	Weight (of water)*
60 x 30 x 30 cm (24 x 12 x 12 in)	55 litres/12 gallons	55 kg/120 lbs
60 x 30 x 38 cm (24 x 12 x 15 in)	68 litres/15 gallons	68 kg/150 lbs
90 x 30 x 30 cm (36 x 12 x 12 in)	82 litres/18 gallons	82 kg/180 lbs
90 x 30 x 38 cm (36 x 12 x 15 in)	104 litres/23 gallons	104kg/230 lbs
120 x 30 x 30 cm (48 x 12 x 12 in)	109 litres/24 gallons	109 kg/240 lbs
120 x 30 x 38 cm (48 x 12x 15 in)	136 litres/30 gallons	136kg/300 lbs

*Don't forget the overall weight will increase when you add in the tank, the stand/cabinet, equipment and furnishings!

Furthermore, the size of the tank will dictate the number of fish – and the size of fish at maturity – that can be housed in comfort.

If we take an example of a 55 litre (12 gallon) tank measuring 60 x 30 x 30 cm (24 x 12 x 12 in):
55 litres dived by 3 (every fish 'needs' 3 litres of water) = 18.

THE SIZE OF A TANK DOES MATTER AND MANY WILL TAKE UP MORE ROOM THAN YOU FIRST THINK BECAUSE YOU NEED A STAND OR UNIT ON WHICH TO PLACE THEM. THESE ARE VERY USEFUL FOR KEEPING VITAL EQUIPMENT SUCH AS TEST KITS AND FOOD, AND FOR 'HIDING' THE WIRING THAT POWERS THE PUMPS, LIGHTS, FILTERS AND HEATERS.

18 is the number of grams of fish for this size tank, but even if a fish weighs only 1–2 grams, they still need room to swim around, they have different body shapes, and they will grow.

A useful additional guide for stocking levels is to use the maximum fish length: for an aquarium between 60–90 cm (24–36 in) long, the maximum total fish length (excluding the caudal fin) is 25 cm (10 in); for an aquarium 120 cm (48 in) long, the maximum total fish length is 38 cm (15 in).

Don't forget that the fish will grow: most are bought as juveniles so expect them to double in size at least and remember, too, that some species need to live in schools while others are happiest as pairs or trios – but there are still some vital preparations to be made before any fish are added to the tank.

DESIGN DECISIONS

There's a huge range of aquarium shapes, sizes and styles to choose from and while any choice will depend of personal preferences, it's the fish that are important and they must be given the right conditions to survive. The best advice is to buy the largest tank you can afford – but also the largest that you can accommodate in your living space. The larger the volume of water a tank holds, the easier it will be to control the waste products that will be deposited in it by the fish and controlling the environment easily means the living conditions for the fish remain more stable. Big volume means temperature changes occur more slowly and any pollution is more diluted.

A good aquarium design will have a large surface area to allow the exchange of gases: remember that like humans, fish breathe in oxygen and exhale carbon dioxide and these gases are dissolved in the water and 'escape' through the surface of the water. In terms of tanks styles, there are cubes, and tanks with curved front 'screens' but you can also get – at a price – different shaped tanks such as hexagonal or 'triangular' shapes designed to fit into corners or very large tanks that can act as 'room dividers' and so you can view the fish 'in the round'. The most popular shape remains the rectangular shaped tank: available in a range of sizes, rectangular tanks give a 'widescreen' format and a nice, large surface area in relation to the volume of water they hold.

TESTING A TANK FOR LEAKS IS VITAL- EVEN A BRAND NEW TANK MAY LEAK AT THE SEAMS AFTER BEING TRANSPORTED HOME. CHECK THE SEAMS CAREFULLY AND REPAIRS IF THEY ARE NEEDED MUST BE MADE ONLY WITH A PROPRIETARY SILICONE SEALANT THAT IS SAFE FOR AQUARIUM LIFE. ORDINARY 'BATHROOM' SEALANTS MUST NOT BE USED AS THESE MAY CONTAIN ANTI-BACTERIAL AGENTS AND SOLVENTS WHICH ARE LETHAL TO FISH.

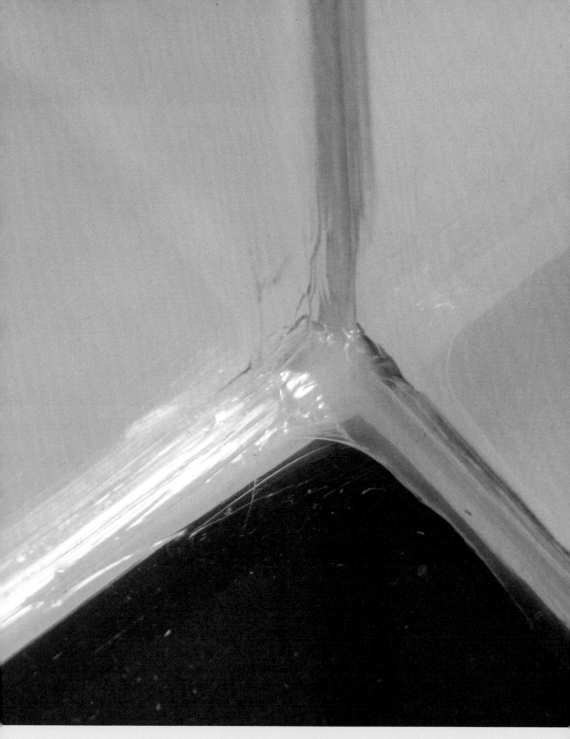

your freshwater aquarium

TANK CONSTRUCTION

Most contemporary tanks are constructed either from a single plastic or acrylic moulding or from five pieces of glass bonded together with a silicone rubber sealant. Sometimes the glass tanks are framed with anodised aluminium or plastic strips: these aren't structural devices but simply to enhance the design. When you buy – and when you get the tank home – check that the seals are not damaged, that there are no scratches on the glass or plastic. Rest the tank on a flat surface while you set up the stand or cabinet: lay some polystyrene tiles on the floor – or even a folded blanket will work – and place the tank gently on top to stop it 'wobbling' and keep it safe. Don't place the tank half on the floor and half on the carpet or rug: the difference in floor levels will cause it to wobble and may crack the glass.

CABINETS AND STANDS

Tanks may come complete with a stand or cabinet or you may buy one separately (some are flat packed for home assembly): cabinets are useful as they can hold all the unsightly power cables and external filters neatly in one place and provide storage for essentials like food that can be kept locked out of reach of children's curiosity! Many cabinets also have integrated hoods with in-built sliding glass trays that act as the condensation tray, shelves for lighting units to rest on and cut-outs at the rear to feed cables through. As in all things: you get what you pay for, but you may be able to find a second hand bargain: beware though that you won't have much redress if the tank turns out to be flawed and leaky.

Whether you choose a stand or a cabinet, you will need assistance setting it up as both are heavy (they need to be able to support the weight of the tank) and they need to be levelled using a spirit level, checking from front to back and side to side. Many stands have adjustable feet so you can keep making adjustments until it's perfect. It sounds obvious, but it's a lot easier to get the stand or cabinet absolutely level before you put the tank on top! And before you put the tank on top of a stand you may also need to prepare a baseboard by cutting a sturdy piece of melamine coated chipboard (cut to fit the stand) and covered with a single layer of polystyrene tiles trimmed to the size of the base of the tank. These provide a level and sturdy base on which the tank will sit happily on the stand. Once again after these have been prepared and 'installed', you'll need to check to make sure it's absolutely level and make adjustments where necessary.

A LARGE RECTANGULAR TANK CAN BECOME THE MAIN FOCUS IN A ROOM AND PROVIDE HOURS OF FASCINATING AND RELAXING VIEWING OF FISH ACTIVITY. THE BASE CABINET FOR EVERY TANK NEEDS TO BE SOLIDLY CONSTRUCTED IN ORDER TO HOLD THE COMBINED WEIGHT OF THE TANK, ITS FURNISHINGS AND THE WATER: ONE LITRE OF WATER WEIGHTS 1 KILOGRAM. THE BASE UNIT CAN ALSO DOUBLE AS STORAGE FOR SPARE EQUIPMENT AND HOUSE OTHERWISE UNSIGHTLY POWER CABLES.

Tip: Always adjust the stand, not the tank! Trying to 'wedge' up a tank to make it level on the stand can cause fractures to the glass.

CLEANING AND TESTING FOR LEAKS

Just because the tank is new, it doesn't mean it's clean! Dust and dirt will have settled on the glass and bottom during storage and transit: leave this here and it'll end up as a film of dirt floating on the surface of the water – a surface that is vital for the passage of oxygen and other gasses. Using a brand new, lint-free cloth and clean water only – no detergents, and not even 'eco' branded washing-up liquid, just plain, clean water – give the inside (and outside) of the tank a clean.

Once the tank is clean, get a friend to help you lift it into position on the stand or cabinet. Once it's in position, check that the whole ensemble is level from side to side and front to back. If necessary make minor adjustments making sure that your helper is holding the tank steady so there's no danger of it fracturing – or worse, falling off the stand.

At this stage it's also worthwhile filling the tank with water to check for leaks: it may be brand new out of the box, but nevertheless, some tanks may have a leak so it's better to find out now rather than later when the fish are installed. If there is a leak, drain out the water and get on the phone to the retailer or supplier. If the tank is second-hand, drain it down, dry it out and reseal it with silicone aquarium sealant. Only use a silicone sealant designed for aquarium use: domestic sealants used in kitchens and bathrooms are not suitable as they contain mildew retardants and fungicides that can be toxic to fish. Once repaired, you can re-test for security, and then start the process of repositioning the tank on the stand once more.

If you are satisfied that there are no leaks from the tank, the next step is to drain out the water! This 'test' water was plain, cold, chlorinated tap water and not good enough quality for fish. Besides, a dry tank is needed to furnish the aquarium with the filter, lighting and heating system. Furthermore, there's the 'aquascape' to create – the substrate and rocks to make the nooks and crannies for the fish to swim in and out of and get it ready for planting.

SECOND HAND AQUARIUM TANKS- PERHAPS SECURED FROM CLUB MEMBERS OR SOURCED FROM LOCAL NEWSPAPERS- ARE OFTEN MUCH CHEAPER THAN NEW TANKS. BUT BEWARE: THESE TANKS MAY LEAK AND CLOSE ATTENTION TO THEIR SEALS IS NEEDED.

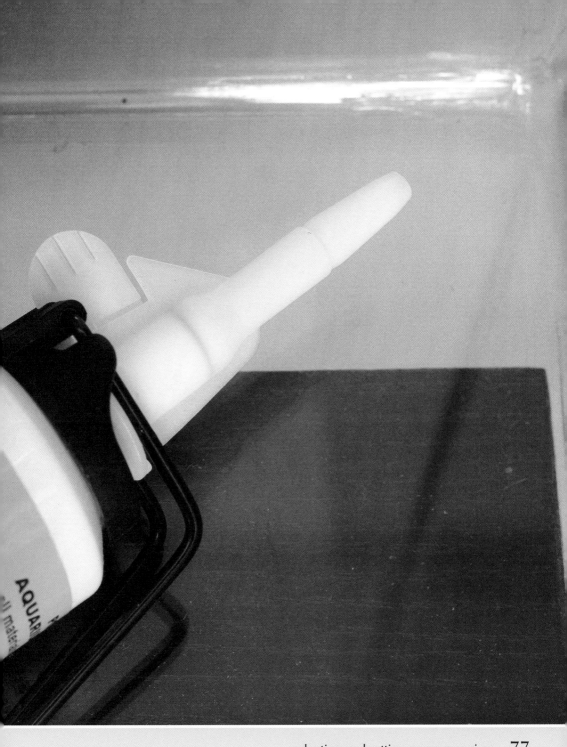

your freshwater aquarium

Essential equipment: heating, lighting, and filtration

The vast majority of fish that will be living in the aquarium will be freshwater tropical species and as their name implies, these fish come from warm tropical waters where the water temperature is around 75°F (24°C) and where the light is more intense and its brightness remains pretty constant for 12 to 14 hours at a time. For these reasons, in order to keep these fish the aquarium water needs to be artificially heated and lit. In addition, filters keep the water clean by removing waste products and keep the pH and hardness of the water in check. A gravel substrate that replicates the natural lake or river bed not only looks good but it provides a medium in which aquatic plants can root and it can also serve as a filtration bed and a spawning site. Some fish, too, like to feed by sifting through the substrate so it is vital for these species to thrive.

SUBSTRATES

To a certain degree, the substrate you choose can be determined by matters of taste: there are natural coloured substrates including black and vivid colour mixes which can look quite gaudy and detract from the natural beauty of the fish. If coloured mixes are used, they should only be purchased from a reputable aquarium supplier to ensure the dye (which may be toxic) doesn't leach out into the water. The bags of gravel that you can find at garden centres for mulching around plants aren't suitable for aquaria: much of this gravel has been dredged up off-shore and will contain quantities of calcium-rich seashells which will harden the water in the tank over time. Aquatic suppliers do sell lime-free gravel, and although it's a bit more expensive than the garden variety, it's worthwhile investing in this to maintain the quality of the water, especially if soft-water inhabiting species are to be kept. The aquatic gravel will also have rounded edges so that the delicate barbells of bottom-dwelling fish aren't damaged.

THE RANGE OF SIZES OF SUBSTRATES- THE MATERIAL THAT COVERS THE BASE OF THE TANK- IS NOT JUST FOR DECORATIVE PURPOSES BUT IS TO REPLICATE THE SEA OR RIVERBED. THIS SUBSTRATE PROVIDES THE ANCHORAGE FOR PLANTS AND FOR SOME SPECIES, A FEEDING GROUND OR A SPAWNING SITE. SPECIALLY PREPARED AQUATIC GRAVEL SHOULD ALWAYS BE USED AS ITS EDGES ARE NICELY ROUNDED SO THEY WON'T CAUSE INJURY TO THE FISH AND CERTAIN GRAVELS ARE AVAILABLE LIME-FREE SO THEY WON'T HARDEN THE WATER IN THE TANK.

Size matters

The particle size of substrates and their composition are important and consideration must be given to the type of filtration unit to be used. Under-gravel filters, which are placed on the floor of the tank and covered by the substrate are not suitable for use with fine sand or fine gravel as the grains fall into and block up the slats in the filter plate.

Tip: If you are using a tank with an under-gravel filter, fit the filter to the base of the tank before you add the gravel!

Fine gravel is suited to small sized aquaria with an internally placed filter and where bigger grains would look out of place. River sand, too, which has rounded grains is ideal for bottom-dwelling species. River sand is non-compacting and so it allows for the free movement of water and plant roots. Again, you could add a small patch of sand to the substrate to make for an interesting and more 'natural' riverbed effect. If you use sand, make sure it is river sand and not sand used in the construction industry and disturb it regularly – but gently (you don't want an underwater sandstorm!) – with your fingers to prevent stagnation.

Coarse gravel, which is suited to larger species of fish also needs special care because it's very easy for debris and decaying matter to get trapped in the spaces between the grains, consequently creating a pollution risk. Additionally, where a biological filter is used, coarse gravel doesn't provide enough surface area for bacteria to colonise and the water flow through the gravel will be too fast. Coarse gravel is best suited to large-scale tanks, but some small amounts mixed with medium sized gravel can still be used to recreate the natural variations of a river bed.

Medium gravel – around 3–5 mm (1/10th–1/5th in) in diameter – is the standard size and provides a suitable substrate for an aquarium of any size. Medium gravel also comes in black, which is ideal for contrasting against brightly coloured species of fish: in the aquarium, the' overhead' light will be reflected up off any light coloured substrate and will make the fish's colours look pale and 'washed out', so a dark coloured substrate enhances the fish's appearance. Furthermore, freshwater fishes usually have a dark-coloured dorsal surface that helps to camouflage them as they swim over dark coloured river beds: in the wild, a fish swimming over a light-coloured river bed would be easily seen by a predator – a bird, fish or an angler.

AQUATIC GRAVEL IS ALSO A GOOD WAY OF DISGUISING FILTRATION UNITS THAT ARE DESIGNED TO BE LOCATED ON THE BED OR FLOOR OF THE TANK. MEDIUM SIZED GRAVEL SHOULD BE USED AS THIS WILL NOT BLOCK THIS TYPE OF FILTER'S VENTS AND IT IS AVAILABLE IN A RANGE OF COLOURS.

your freshwater aquarium

How deep to go

The amount of substrate you will need will of course depend on the size of your tank and whether or not you are using an under-gravel filter. If you are using a 'normal' filter then the substrate should be 4–5 cm (1.5–2 in) deep; where an under-gravel filter is used the substrate needs to be about 6 cm (2.5 in) deep. In parts of the tank you can of course do a bit of 'aquascaping': maintain the minimum depths at all times and add additional substrate material to create contours so there are different heights to the 'river bed'. Remember too that the substrate is also where the aquatic plants' roots are anchored, so the substrate needs to be deep enough to keep them in place.

Wash away

Sand and gravel may have been washed before it left the quarry but it's not clean enough to go straight into the aquarium and must be washed thoroughly. Place a small amount of the sand or gravel in a bucket, add some clean water and agitate it – use your hands or even str it with a wooden spoon to get the water all over it. Drain off the dirty water and keep repeating until the water runs clear. When this happens, that batch of substrate is nice and clean and ready to go into the tank.

Add the gravel slowly and gently to the base of the tank using your hands or a small plastic bowl – don't use metal or ceramic containers just in case you drop it into the tank and crack the glass! As you add the gravel, you can spread it around over the base and 'landscape' it: some aquarists like to slope the substrate upwards towards the rear of the tank – like a raked theatre stage. This is fine, but it's a good idea to build up the 'zones' at the left and right edges of the tank a little for the planting and always re-member the minimum depth of substrate at the front and middle of the tank that is needed for the type of filter you have.

Nutritional supplements

Most aquarium substrates such as sand and gravel don't contain any nutrients and on their own can-not sustain the life of plants. To improve the growing conditions for the plants in the aquarium, you can add nutrient – plant food – directly to the substrate. Some of these supplements need to be used in con-junction with a bacterial culture that will act on the food and release it in a form that the plants can absorb. Sprinkle the supplement over the surface of the gravel and if a bacterial culture is used, this should be crumbled up and added as a thin layer on top of the supplement. Next, gently mix the two into the substrate with your fingers, smooth over the top and if necessary, add a final sprinkling of sub-strate to ensure the level is correct. The nutritional supplement will sustain the aquatic plants for sev-eral months: after this time, you will need to add 'fertiliser' in tablet form positioned close to the roots of the plants to keep on feeding them.

TAKE CARE WHEN ADDING SUBSTRATES TO THE TANK DURING FURNISHING SO
THAT THEY DON'T SCRATCH THE TANK'S WALLS.

FILTERS

To keep the water in an aquarium clean and the fish healthy, a filter is vital. Many modern filters not only clean the water of suspended waste material, some are also designed to maintain the right pH and hardness or softness of the water. Depending on their design, filters can operate mechanically, chemically or biologically. The last method of filtration is increasingly the most popular and widespread method. Additionally, filters may be internal or external. Unless your tank is large – around 180 litres (40 gallons) – an internal power filter that sits in the rear of the tank will work well. But it's worth bearing in mind that it is always better to use a slightly larger and more powerful filter than the one recommended for your tank size.

How filters work

Internal power filters are composed of a submersible water pump at the top of the filter unit. Powered by a small electric motor, the pump draws water through the filter medium – a piece of foam that acts as a sponge and also allows good bacteria to colonise – and circulates the water back through the tank. As the water is pumped back into the tank, it is aerated by a venturi pipe that accelerates the water flow and draws in a stream of air from above the surface of the water. Aeration increases the amount of oxygen in the water and the agitation of the water it produces also drives carbon dioxide from the water by pushing it to the water surface. While there are different models of internal power filters on the market, they all operate on the same principles. It's a good idea to look for one with a venturi pipe fitted.

Filter medium: good bacteria

The filter medium is generally a block of foam that provides a large area for beneficial bacteria to colonise. The good bacteria in the tank are the Nitrosomonas that break down ammonia (produced by fish from the gills during their respiration and in their faeces) and convert it into the less harmful (but still toxic) nitrites. These are hoovered up by the bacteria Nitrobacter and turned into nitrate that is used by the plants in the aquarium as food. Not all of the nitrates will be utilised, so the aquarium keeper still needs to remove some water in the tank and replace it with fresh water on a regular basis.

While the bacteria break down much of the waste matter produced by the fish, some filters also have another container to hold additional cleansers such as activated carbon that further filter the dissolved waste products from fish, uneaten food and decaying plant material. It's important to note that the activated carbon will also filter out any medication that may be added to the water if the fish are show-

A RANGE OF DIFFERENT SIZES AND TYPES OF FILTERS ARE AVAILABLE: THESE INCLUDE MECHANICAL AND CHEMICAL FILTERS, ALTHOUGH BIOLOGICAL FILTERS ARE INCREASINGLY POPULAR. FURTHERMORE, SOME FILTERS ARE INTERNAL OR EXTERNAL, BUT EITHER WAY, IT'S ALWAYS A GOOD IDEA TO USE A POWERED FILTER THAT IS SUITED TO A TANK THAT IS A BIT LARGER THAN THE ONE YOU HAVE.

your freshwater aquarium

ing signs of ill health: during the treatment phase the carbon filter should be removed, but the main filter left running to maintain water quality and aeration – especially as some fish treatments can reduce the level of oxygen in the water.

No moving parts: under-gravel filters

There are also biological under-gravel filters that sit, as their name suggests, on the base of the fish tank underneath the gravel substrate. These filters don't have any moving parts and require little maintenance beyond stirring up the gravel to help remove the detritus. It's vital, however, that the correct depth – and size of grain – of substrate is used so the slats in the filter don't get blocked up, and that the filter covers the entire base of the tank with no gaps or spaces at the edges. With this type of filtration system, a separate aeration unit is needed to agitate the water surface that lets it absorb oxygen from the atmosphere. Run by a small electric pump, air is drawn in through a one-way valve into a tube feeding the tank and is fed through an air stone that releases the air in a stream of tiny bubbles from the bottom of the tank.

External power filters

These are generally larger than the internal versions and are housed outside the tank, often in the cabinet space beneath the tank. They too can be mechanical, biological or chemical filters and provide the same services. The only difference is that because they are located outside of the tank, there is more room in the tank and they don't have to be hidden behind plants to make them aesthetically pleasing.

Filter installation and maintenance

Internal power filters are easy to install: follow the manufacturer's instructions and make sure that all plastic wrapping is removed – and check, too, that the filter foam inserts are there. Assemble the filter and sit it in the plastic cradle supplied:

• The cradle is attached to the interior glass wall at the rear corner of the tank by suction cups – it's a good idea to have some spares and you may need to dampen the cups a little to get them to stick.
• Position the filter with the nozzle facing outwards so that you have directed the oxygenated outflow of water diagonally across the tank for optimum aeration.
• The head of the filter should sit just below the water's surface (but check the manufacturer's installation instructions for precise measurements).

INTERNAL POWERED FILTERS NEED TO BE POSITIONED AT THE BACK OF THE TANK, IN A REAR CORNER AND HELD AGAINST THE TANK WALLS WITH SUCTION CUPS. THE FILTER NOZZLE NEEDS TO BE FACING OUTWARDS SO THE OXYGENATED FLOW OF WATER MOVES DIAGONALLY ACROSS THE TANK.

• Make sure there is a gap between the base of the filter and the top of the substrate to avoid any build-up of dirt and debris and to allow the free passage of water around and into the filter.

You also need to make sure that the power cable is long enough to reach the power source, and it's vital that you can access the filter itself easily because you will need to maintain it regularly. When water renovation is carried out – 20–25% of the old water is removed and replaced with fresh – this is also the time to rinse the filter medium foam: use the water you have removed from the tank. This ensures that the good bacteria aren't cleaned away, but will remove any big bits of debris that may be clogging the pores in the foam.

Clean all parts of the filter using the aquarium water and wipe with some filter wool, making sure that there are no slithers of plants stuck in any slots. If your filter has a compartment for activated carbon, then replace this too. Place the new batch of carbon in a fine mesh sieve and rinse it well under cold running water. Once the filter is clean, reassemble it and replace it in the tank: make sure the unit floods with water fully as any air trapped inside will stop it working properly. Every six months or so, it's a good idea to replace half of the filter foam. Wait one month to replace the other half of the foam to allow the good bacteria time to colonise the new foam.

Tip: Replace half of the filter foam when it no longer returns to its original shape after you have squeezed it!

Tip: Keep the manufacturer's assembly instructions in a safe place: this means that when you disassemble the filter canister for cleaning and then reassemble it, it will be in the correct manner.

Warning: Never run the filter pump when it's out of water: you will burn out the motor. If you want to test-run the filter, submerge it a bucket of water.

AN UNDER GRAVEL FILTER (LEFT) HAS NO MOVING PARTS, BUT DOES NEED TO HAVE ITS VENTS KEPT CLEAN OF DEBRIS AND GRAVEL SUBSTRATE NEEDS TO BE OF A GOOD SIZE SO NOT TO BLOCK THE VENTS. ALSO, YOU WILL STILL NEED TO PROVIDE A SEPARATE AERATION UNIT TO PROVIDE OXYGEN. ALL PARTS NEED TO BE KEPT CLEAN (RIGHT) USING AQUARIUM WATER AND WIPING OFF DEBRIS WITH FILTER WOOL. EXTERNAL FILTER BOXES (BELOW) ARE GENERALLY LARGER THAN INTERNAL UNITS AND CAN BE HOUSED IN THE BASE UNITS OR CABINETS OF TANKS, THEREBY FREEING UP VALUABLE TANK SPACE.

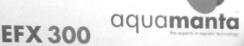

EFX 300

aquamanta
the experts in aquatic technology

What makes Canister Filters better than in tank filters (Internal Filters)?
Due to the pressurised seal, Canister Filters are able to clean deeper, resulting in cleaner, healthier water.

Where do I locate the Canister Filter?
The filter is designed to go under the aquarium in your cabinet, hence it does not take up valuable space in the aquarium.

Do canister filters come in different sizes for different aquariums?
Yes they do, see the table below for a guide to the range.
Within the Aquamanta range there is a whole world of quality products for your aquarium, for more information see your Aquamanta retailer.

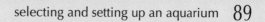

your freshwater aquarium

HEATING THE WATER

In the wild, tropical fish inhabit waters whose temperatures are around 23–27°C (73–80°F). In the aquarium, most will live happily in water that's a pleasant 24°C (75°F). To achieve and maintain this temperature constantly, the aquarium needs a combined heater and thermostat – known as a heater-stat. Once set to the required temperature and switched on, the heaterstat will heat the aquarium water to the right warmth and then switch itself on and off in order to keep the temperature stable. There will be minor fluctuations in temperature, but these will take place slowly. It is important that the appropriate size of heater – which is measured in watts – is used in the corresponding size tank. Too large a heater will cause rapid rises in temperature, which can be fatal to fish; too small a heater and it will have to work extra hard and will burn out pretty fast.

As a general rule, allow 50 watts for every 27 litres (6 gallons) of water, so a tank measuring 60 x 30 x 30 cm (24 x 12 x 12 in) that holds 55 litres (12 gallons) would require a 100-watt heater (see the table of tank volumes on page 71). For a large tank, it's worth considering investing in two heaters to share the total wattage between them, with each being controlled by its own thermostat. If one heater fails, the other will at least keep the temperature of the water up to a safe level until you can undertake a repair or replacement.

Installing a heaterstat

Heaterstats are very easy to install but, once again, check that the power cable is long enough to reach the power source. Unpack it and read the instructions: different models may have their temperature scales calibrated in centigrade or fahrenheit, so make sure you know what the temperature equivalents are. Check to see if the temperature has been set at a default setting and alter it as required. Some models recommend that they are placed at an angle with the heating element at the bottom so the heat rises and doesn't go straight past the thermostat. Leave a small gap between the bottom of the heaterstat and the substrate – don't be tempted to cover it with gravel because this will cause it to overheat – and make sure that any tank furnishings are not placed too close to the heaterstat or they will obstruct the flow of water. Most heaterstats are stick-like or rod-shaped designs: once again these are positioned in a rear corner and attached to the aquarium glass with suckers.

Some heaterstat models have a small light that tells you they are working: if your model has this option, make sure you can see it easily.

HEATERSTATS ARE A COMBINED HEATER AND THERMOSTAT AND ARE DESIGNED TO KEEP THE WATER TEMPERATURE IN A TANK AT AN OPTIMUM 24° C (75° F). THE HEATER HEATS THE WATER TO THE SET TEMPERATURE AND THE THERMOSTAT SWITCHES THE HEATER OFF WHEN THE TEMPERATURE IS REACHED- AND ON AGAIN WHEN THE TEMPERATURE DROPS SO ANY FLUCTUATIONS IN TEMPERATURE ARE KEPT TO A MINIMUM.

Take the temperature

While the heaterstat will do its job, it's still vital that the aquarium keeper monitors temperature in the tank. Temperature checks should be made twice a day using an internal or an external thermometer attached to the tank. Internal thermometers should be attached (by the sucker) to a top front corner of the tank well away from the current of a power filter. Digital thermometers that stick on the outside of the glass are popular.

In addition to these combined heaterstats, there are also submersible heating cables and mats that work like underfloor heating in houses. Just like the under-gravel filters, these heaters lie underneath the gravel substrate, so need to be installed before you lay the substrate. The drawback with these heating systems is that they need to be controlled by a separate thermostat, either submerged in the tank or externally located.

Warning! Don't switch on the heaterstat if it is not submerged in water; it will burn out. If you want to test it, submerge it in a bucket of water.
Emergency! If the heaterstat stops working – when there is a power cut for example – don't panic. Severe temperature loss won't happen for several hours and you can take immediate action by wrapping the aquarium in some sheets of polystyrene, a blanket or in thick layers of newspaper. If the temperature in the aquarium is falling to critical levels, then fill some plastic bottles with hot water and float them in the tank!

LET THERE BE LIGHT!

Aquarium lights not only illuminate the underwater world so we can admire the beauty of the fish, but also stimulate fish activity and enable the aquatic plants to photosynthesise. If we remember that plants 'breathe in' carbon dioxide during daylight hours and 'exhale' oxygen during the night, we can see how light is vital in the aquarium for maintaining a stable level of dissolved gases that can support the other underwater life. Tropical fish come from regions where day and night are almost equal in length, so for life in the aquarium to flourish the tank needs to be lit for between 10 and 15 hours a day.

WATER TEMPERATURE CONTROL IS VITAL - SOME TROPICAL FISH WILL MATE AND SPAWN ONLY WHEN THE WATER REACHES A PARTICULAR TEMPERATURE- WHAT WOULD HAPPEN NATURALLY IN THE WILD WITH SEASONS. DIGITAL THERMOMETERS (LEFT) THAT ADHERE TO THE OUTSIDE OF THE TANK ARE A USEFUL 'AT A GLANCE' DEVICE, BUT IDEALLY SHOULD BE SUPPLEMENTED WITH AN IN-TANK THERMOMETER AS THESE ARE MORE ACCURATE. LIGHTS (RIGHT) NOT ONLY ALLOW US TO SEE THE FISH IN THEIR FULL GLORY, BUT ARE USED TO REPLICATE THE NATURAL DAY AND NIGHT CYCLES OF FISH KEPT IN TANKS: FOR US TO ENJOY THEM AT OUR LEISURE- IN THE EVENINGS PERHAPS- THE NATURAL DAYTIME OF FISH CAN BE MANIPULATED BY TIMER SWITCHES.

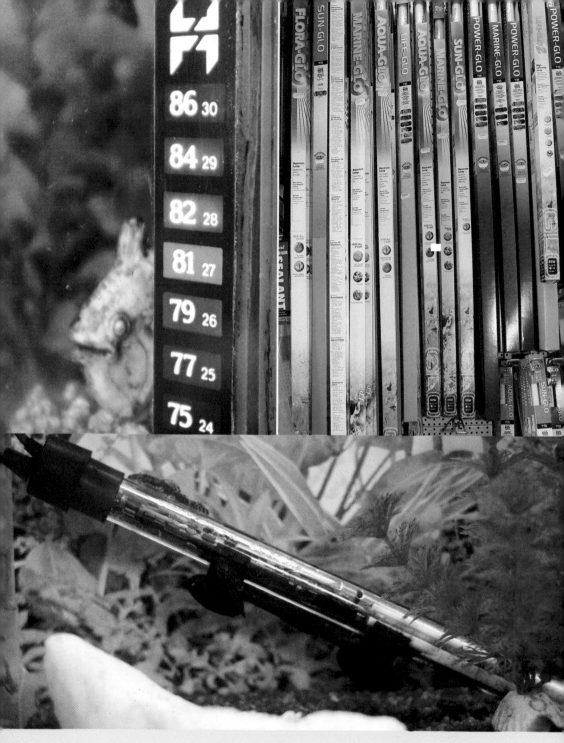

When to light

Just like humans, fish need the regular cycle of day and night: although they don't sleep, fish do enter a sleep-like state at night. The aquarium keeper will no doubt want to enjoy the scene when he or she is at home in the evening, so in the aquarium, the human daytime becomes the fish night. This is easily achieved by using an automatic timer to switch the tank lights on and off at preset times. Nevertheless, it's important that there is some light in the room in which the tank is located: this will avoid the shock and dramatic change of the sudden on or off light situations that are distressing to fish.

Many aquaria come complete with integrated lighting systems concealed under the decorative hood of the tank. The hood not only finishes off the look of the aquarium, but also keeps out dirt and debris – and interfering fingers (and paws). It also stops fish from jumping out of the tank! Different designs of hood have different fittings for the lights – some have clips into which the lamps fit, others have a shelf that the lamp sits on – so read the instructions for fitting.

Lighting types

Bulb-shaped high intensity lights mounted in individual reflectors are excellent for very deep tanks because they allow the keeper to spotlight different areas or features of the tank. They are, however, expensive and they do produce a lot of extra heat. More usual are fluorescent tube lights that are housed in the hood of the tank: these long-running lamps are 'cool' and provide an even distribution of light – and they are available in different colours to enhance the appearance of the fish and promote plant growth. You can use the fluorescent tubes in different colour combinations: a bright cold white tube alongside a warmer pink-coloured light covers the full light spectrum and will show the fish's colours beautifully. The inside surface of the tank hood should be white to reflect the light back into the tank.

Fitting and replacing the bulbs

Fitting the bulbs is straightforward, if a little fiddly. The bulb ends with their prongs need to be aligned with the holding clips. Take care not to use too much force or you'll break the clips – and possibly the bulb. Feed any of the leads through the holes at the rear of the hood and make sure the end caps are fitted tightly to the end of the bulb. Don't cut away any of the end cap to make the fitting easier: these have a plastic collar to make a watertight seal that is essential in an aquarium. All light bulbs have a limited life span and although they might still look bright, aquarium bulbs should be replaced every 12–18 months. When you fit the bulbs – or replace them – get a friend to hold open the hood lid so it doesn't drop down as you work.

FLUORESCENT TUBES MOUNTED OVER THE TOP OF THE TANK ARE THE MOST COMMON METHOD OF LIGHTING THE TANK BECAUSE THEY ARE 'COOL' RUNNING SO ADD NO HEAT TO THE TANK AND EVENLY DISTRIBUTE THE LIGHT. ADDITIONALLY THEY ARE AVAILABLE IN A RANGE OF TONES AND COLOURS TO REFLECT AND ENHANCE THE FISH'S COLOURS.

Tip: Overheating can occur in summer hot spells, causing loss of oxygen in the water and problems for the fish. On such days, switch off the lights and use a small electric fan near to the tank to keep it cool and ensure maximum ventilation.

Warning: Water and electricity don't mix! Always switch off the electrical supply and unplug any device before undertaking aquarium maintenance.

CONDENSATION TRAY

The final major piece of essential aquarium kit is a condensation tray – some tanks have these integrated into the hood. Condensation trays are transparent sliding covers situated between the tank and the lighting unit. They are designed to help minimise evaporation and they also stop the condensation from settling on electrical components housed in the tank hood. Because they are made of clear plastic, or glass, the condensation trays don't interfere with the amount of light entering the tank. They do, however, need to be kept clean at all times: dirty trays – caused by bits of spilled fish food, build-up of salts created by condensation and algae growth – will reduce the light in the tank. This will impact on the health of the plants and ultimately of the fish.

Make sure the condensation trays are in place before you fit the hood onto the aquarium. Remember the hood may be quite heavy – especially if it has fluorescent tubes in it. Get someone to help you position the hood; you don't want to drop it and crack the trays or the tank!

With all of the essentials in place it's now time to do a bit of aquatic landscaping and then the 'elixir of life' – water – can be added to the aquarium. The next section deals with the types of rocks, woods and other furnishings that are suited to tropical freshwater aquaria. It explains how to make them ready for the tank, how the aquarium is 'run in' and which aquatic plants can be used to bring the aquascape to life.

AQUARIUM LIGHTS ARE USUALLY HOUSED IN THE 'LIDS' OF TANKS AND SEPARATED FROM THE WATER BY A CONDENSATION TRAY. THE BULBS WILL NEED REGULAR INSPECTION AND REPLACING AND EVERY TIME ROUTINE MAINTENANCE IS UNDERTAKEN IN THE TANK, THE LIGHTS SHOULD BE SWITCHED OFF FOR SAFETY.

aquascaping

Creating an effective underwater display that goes some way towards replicating the features that are to be found in the fish's natural habitat not only looks attractive to the human eye, but also means that the tank inhabitants will not become stressed or unhealthy. In the wild, rocky outcrops, sunken logs, twisted roots and plants provide the fish with nooks and crannies in which to rest and avoid their predators, so furnishing the aquarium with similar features allows the fish to live according to their instinctive behaviour. Some fish like to hide in caves and some secrete themselves among the plants, but other species enjoy being out in the open, so swimming spaces must be left in both the upper and lower regions of the tank.

Natural looks nice

Like multicoloured Day-Glo gravel – which can detract from the natural beauty of the fish's colours and patterns – the choice of furnishings for a tropical freshwater aquarium can be guided by maters of taste. A fairy grotto or a sunken, plastic submarine may entertain you, but the fish may well be suspicious of such objects and avoid them. The intention of the true aquarist is to replicate a biotope in which the fish will be happy, so in most instances, natural furnishings such as rocks and wood work the best.

TANK BACKGROUNDS

You can buy backgrounds for your aquarium that stick to the outside glass of the rear wall: these come in a range of styles including plain colours (black shows off the fish's colours), images of ancient submerged ruins or trompe l'oeil (fools the eye) images of a naturalistic underwater scene. A background will not only make your interior display appear larger than it really is, but also hide any cables dangling from the tank – or even wallpaper that may be behind it and visible through the glass!

BEWARE FALLING ROCKS!

At first glance, it's easy to imagine that rocks vary only in size, shape and colour and that any attractive rock can be placed in the aquarium. However, the fish in the tank will be living in very close proximity to these rocky features, so they should have no sharp or jagged edges – and avoid creating a precarious tower of rocks that could collapse. An avalanche might fracture the tank, trap and injure fish and, if we recall that fish are very sensitive to vibrations, cause them great distress. If you want to create a tall outcrop feature of individual rocks, it's best to arrange them first, deciding on the shape and size of the structure, and then glue them together with a silicone sealant suitable for aquarium use.

TANK BACKGROUNDS ARE A USEFUL WAY OF ADDING 'DEPTH' TO THE TANK: THEY COME IN A RANGE OF SIZES AND ATTRACTIVE UNDERWATER SCENES AND STICK TO THE OUTSIDE OF THE REAR WALL OF THE TANK. THEY ARE ALSO USEFUL FOR HIDING CABLES THAT MIGHT OTHERWISE BE VISIBLE- AND EVEN THE WALLPAPER IN YOUR HOME!

Chemistry

Understanding how the mineral composition of rocks placed in the aquarium affects the chemical composition of the water – and in turn the fish – is also important. Rocks that are soluble (dissolve in water), particularly those that are calcareous (chalky, or containing calcium carbonate), should not be used in a freshwater aquarium where a soft water environment is required. Limestone and crumbly stone, such as sandstone, or any rocks that contain metal ore are likewise not suitable for the aquarium. While a piece of natural coral may look attractive, it too is calcareous and should not be used in the freshwater aquarium. Coral is also extremely sharp and can cut fish (and keepers). Furthermore, the coral reefs that provide it are living organisms that are under threat from pollution and climate change and need protecting.

Let's rock!

Rocks that are suited to the aquarium include granite, basalt, quartz and slate, not only for their 'inert' qualities – they won't alter the pH or hardness of the water – but also because they can be used for their decorative effects. The rocks will come in a range of different colours: dark slate provides dramatic contrast against the fish's colours and golden brown rock glows beautifully under the tank's illumination. Weathered rock will have lots of interesting natural features to create textures in the tank.

Preparing rocks

Your aquarium supplier will stock a range of rocks suitable for the freshwater aquarium: check with them to make sure you have selected rocks with the right chemistry for your tank because there are other rocks – such as tufa – with different chemical structures that are used in aquaria. Choose a range of sizes – a few large angular shaped rocks and some medium and smaller smooth, water-worn stones and pebbles for variety – for you and the fish. The next step is to get scrubbing! Get an old, but clean, nail brush and a toothbrush (for getting into the small nooks) and scrub away with clean, lukewarm water (not detergents) to remove the dirt, dust, debris and any moss or lichens on the rocks. You don't want dirt fouling your aquarium water, so remove it well.

Placing in the tank

Once clean, the rocks can be placed in the aquarium – that still doesn't contain any water! This is a bit like being a theatre director: you are positioning props on the stage so the actors (in this case, the fish) can move around them. Keep checking on the position of key features in the tank by standing back and looking at the set from the front and side walls. Place the larger features at the rear of the tank and smaller ones at the front. A useful layout of elements is one used by painters of still-lifes:

The elevation – the view from the front – of all the objects appears like an off-centre triangle...

... with some tall objects to one side, while arrangement of the objects on the plan – seen from overhead – are arranged across a parallelogram:

Place the imaginary off-centre triangle on the parallelogram (here the aquarium walls) – it doesn't have to be straight on – and see the effect. If you want, make a sketch of the tank and block in the heaterstat and filter in the rear corners and then arrange some cutout pieces of paper around the tank to get an idea of the placement of rocks and other furnishings.

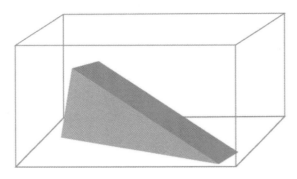

THE DWARF GOURAMI (TOP) IS THE SMALLEST OF THE THREE GOURAMI SPECIES WHOSE NATIVE HABITAT IS INDIA, ESPECIALLY INDIA AND BENGAL. IT IS QUIET A SHY FISH AND PEACEFUL BY NATURE SO T MAY BE KEPT IN A COMMUNITY TANK OF FISH OF SIMILAR SIZE 3.8- 4 CM (1 ½ IN) WITH LOTS OF PLANTING IN WHICH IT CAN HIDE IF IT FEELS BULLIED.
BELOW: UNDERSTANDING THE COMPOSITION OF ROCKS THAT ARE DESTINED FOR THE AQUARIUM IS VITAL AS THEIR MINERAL CONTENT MAY ALTER THE EATER CHEMISTRY. GRANITE, BASALT, QUARTZ AND SLATE ARE IDEAL ROCK FURNISHINGS BECAUSE THEY ARE INERT.

This arrangement gives a pleasing composition that the eye follows forwards and backwards, rather than in a straight line across the front of the aquarium. You can balance the heights at the other side with some tall plants. Play around with the key elements until you are happy with how they look.

Tip: Remember that the power filter located in one of the back corners of the tank has its output angled so the aerated water flows diagonally across the tank from front to back. The aerated outflow should not be halted by a large object like a rock placed dead centre in the tank: arrange the furnishings so there's a gently winding corridor through which the aerated water can snake. (The diagram above presumes the filter is positioned in the rear right-hand corner.)

Tip: For a really natural look, position all the rocks so that their strata run in the same direction.

Tip: Remember to leave enough room so you can service the equipment and the tank easily: you can hide the filter and heaterstat behind rocks and plants but remember to leave enough space around the equipment so their work is not interrupted.

Take care positioning the rocks so you don't bang them against the tank walls or floor. When you have decided on the position of the key feature rocks, wiggle the rocks into the substrate so they sit right on the floor of the tank: this way, the fish won't undermine the rocks and cause them to become unstable or shift position in the tank. Use the smaller rocks and pebbles to create additional features.

ALL THE FURNISHING IN THE TANK NEEDS TO BE THOROUGHLY CLEANED BEFORE THEY ARE PLACED IN POSITION: THIS INCLUDES GRAVEL SUBSTRATES AND LARGER ROCKS AND THESE SHOULD BE SCRUBBED CLEAN AND RINSED WITH CLEAN WATER. POSITION ROCKS CAREFULLY IN THE TANK SO YOU DON'T SCRATCH OR SHATTER THE GLASS AND THEN WIGGLE THEM INTO THE SUBSTRATE SO THEY SIT RIGHT ON THE FLOOR OF THE TANK: THIS WAY FISH WON'T UNDERMINE THEM AND BRING THEM TOPPLING DOWN.

your freshwater aquarium

WOOD

In addition to rocks, cork bark, driftwood, twisted roots and bogwood can all be used to create a natural looking environment. While you can collect these yourself from rivers, marshes and forests, you must ensure that any wood is absolutely dead and has no traces of rot. You also need to make sure that there are no earwigs, beetles or beetle larvae hidden in it! It's often simpler just to buy the wood from the aquarium supplier: this is the best way to avoid introducing any pollutants to the tank. Cork is easy to cut into shape and some pieces look as though they have been torn straight from the tree bark, which gives a very pleasing effect.

Cork, of course, floats, so it needs to be thoroughly soaked in water to make it waterlogged. You can use cork floor or wall tiles, but make sure they have not been sealed or varnished or backed onto hardboard: the glues, sealants and varnishes may be toxic to the fish. Attach a dry piece of cork to a piece of slate using a silicone sealant designed for aquarium use, then bury the slate 'anchor' in the substrate to stop the cork floating away.

Bogwood – long-dead roots that have been preserved in boggy conditions – are very popular but will leach tannins into the water and colour it brown. Before bogwood – or any other pieces of wood you select – is used it must be cleaned by boiling it several times in changes of water until there is no sign of any discolouration. In cold water, give all the pieces of a wood a good scrub to remove any dirt and debris from nooks and crannies.

Getting the wood really wet also gives you the opportunity to make sure that it sinks. It's worthwhile testing that your piece of wood sinks before you add water to the tank – otherwise it will float to the surface. It's air in the wood that makes it float, so place the wood in a bucket of clean water and let it soak up the water and expel any air: you might need to leave it overnight. If the wood doesn't sink in the bucket, it won't sink in the aquarium, so your only alternative is to let it dry out and then attach it to a slate or pebble anchor with silicone sealant designed for aquarium use.

If, at this stage, you're not prepared to scrub your wood clean, then you could always opt for imitation logs and roots designed for use in the aquarium that are closely modelled on the real thing. These soon become covered in a coating of algae, making it difficult to tell whether they are real or not.

PIECES OF CLEANED DRIFTWOOD AND BOGWOOD MAKE ATTRACTIVE UNDERWATER
FEATURES AND PROVIDE NOOKS AND CRANNIES FOR FISH TO EXPLORE AND IN
WHICH TO REST.

Size and shape

The size and shape of the wood pieces you use are up to you: in the shop, try holding some pieces up against a similar sized tank to yours to see whether the size and shape are right for your needs. Check over the wood you buy carefully and avoid any pieces with sawn-off edges as these look unnatural in the tank. Look at the wood for its graining patterns and its shape: pieces that look like a tree root should be used similarly; they'll look odd if you try to make a branch out of them! Don't forget, because there's no water in your tank, you can take your time playing around with arrangements until you are completely satisfied with the overall effect. When you've decided on the position, wriggle the wood well into the substrate.

Warning! Don't place any wood in front of the filter or you will block the flow of water.

Tip: Wood furnishings are great ways to disguise the presence of the heaterstat, but it is vital that the wood does not rest against it, because the heaterstat could then overheat.

BEFORE THEY CAN BE ADDED TO THE TANK, PIECES OF WOOD NEED TO BE SCRUBBED CLEAN, RINSED WELL AND THEN SOAKED TO FILL ANY AIR HOLES WITH WATER SO THET WILL SINK AND SETTLE AT THE BOTTOM OF THE TANK. ANY PIECES THAT INSIST ON FLOATING CAN BE ANCHORED TO A PIECE OF SLATE BURIED UNDER THE SUBSTRATE.

your freshwater aquarium

Adding the vital water

Once all the hard furnishings are in place, you can add the vital ingredient of water to your tank. If you don't already know the type of water you have in your home – its pH level and its hardness or softness – then you need to find out now! Go back to Chapter 2 to remind yourself of the importance of understanding the water chemistry in order to keep tropical freshwater fish.

CONDITIONING THE WATER

If you have tested your tap water for pH and hardness, you can now 'wash it': you'll need to add a proprietary water conditioner to remove any chemicals like chlorine that are harmful to fish. Read and follow the manufacturer's instructions carefully and use a large bucket – find out how much it can hold. Fill the bucket with cold tap water and then add the required amount of 'cleanser' for the volume.

Keep a record of the number of buckets you have used to fill the tank. The volumes of rectangular aquarium tanks given earlier (see page 71) were for empty tanks – no rocks, no substrate, no bits of wood, no filters or heaterstats, which all displace water, were included. With all the furnishings in place, the volume of water needed to fill the tank to the correct level will be much less. Knowing exactly how much water is required is vital for future reference: many medications for treating sick fish in the aquarium are diluted according to the volume of water in the tank, and not its empty capacity.

FILLING UP

Use a jug to transfer the cleaned water to the aquarium: it's the simplest way to fill the tank. It may take a while longer, but using a jug to fill a tank has its benefits: by pouring the water from the jug slowly over a flat stone you will avoid disturbing and stirring up the substrate – and possibly dislodging any wooden features or revealing your anchor slates. If there isn't a suitable flat stone in your aquarium display, then you can improvise: pour the water into a shallow saucer or small plate placed on the substrate instead. The cleaner your gravel substrate was to begin with, the less likely it will make the water cloudy as you add water. If you were a bit slack at the substrate stage, then your lack of cleaning will be very visible!

ONCE ALL THE FURNISHINGS ARE IN PLACE, WATER CAN BE ADDED. SO THAT WOOD AND ROCKS ARE NOT DISLODGED WITH SAND OR DUST FROM GRAVEL SUBSTRATES SWIRLED AROUND (CLOUDING THE WATER), WATER SHOULD BE POURED IN VERY GENTLY USING A JUG.

Once you have filled the aquarium to a level where the water is well above the level of the substrate – perhaps halfway up your largest rock feature – then you can switch to filling up with a bucket, but again, this must be done slowly and gently. Once the aquarium is full, carefully rearrange any disturbed substrate (caused by over-vigorous pouring).

Turning on and running in the system

At this stage, the water level in the aquarium can be about 2.5 cm (1 incn) below the final level (you can top it up later) but it must cover the heaterstat and the filter to the recommended levels.

At this stage, too, you might think you can start adding some aquatic plants or even some fish. Unfortunately, this is not so: the system needs to be checked and run in, and the water temperature and quality brought up to optimum levels. Running in the system is best done over a 24-hour period. This lets you check and adjust the operations of the filter and the heaterstat and is a lot easier to do without plant fronds clinging to your arm! It also allows time for the water to heat up enough: the aquatic plants – like tropical fish – won't get off to a good start in their new home if they are plunged into icy water. Waiting at least another 24 hours also allows you to think about which plants and (later) which fish you'd like to live in your aquarium.

LEFT: ONCE THE TANK HAS BEEN FILLED WELL ABOVE THE SUBSTRATE LEVEL- AND ABOUT HALF WAY UP THE LARGEST ROCK OF WOOD FEATURE- YOU CAN POUR WATER IN WITH A LARGER VESSEL. THE WATER LEVEL MUST COVER THE HEATERSTAT AND FILTER TO THE LEVELS RECOMMENDED ON THE DEVICES.

RIGHT: ALTHOUGH THE TANK IS FULL OF WATER IT IS BY NO MEANS READY TO RECEIVE ANY FISH: THERE IS STILL PLENTY OF PREPARATORY WORK TO DO AND AFTERWARDS, REGULAR ROUTINE INSPECTION AND CLEANING WILL BE REQUIRED.

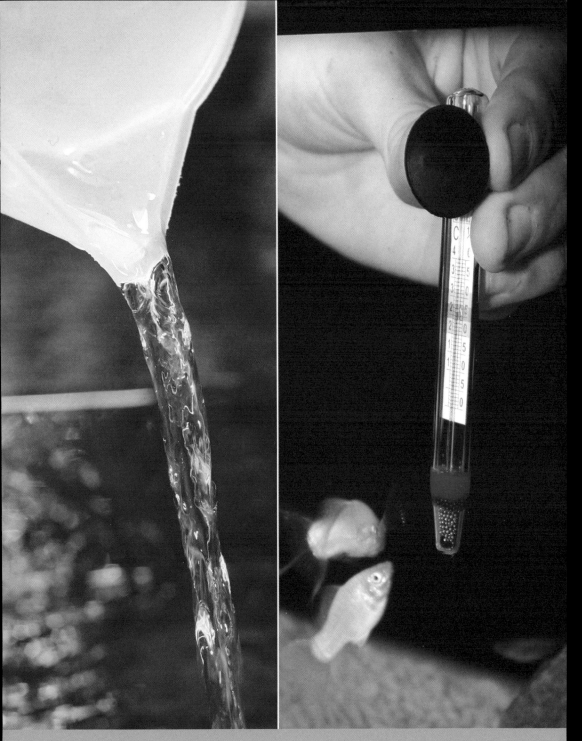

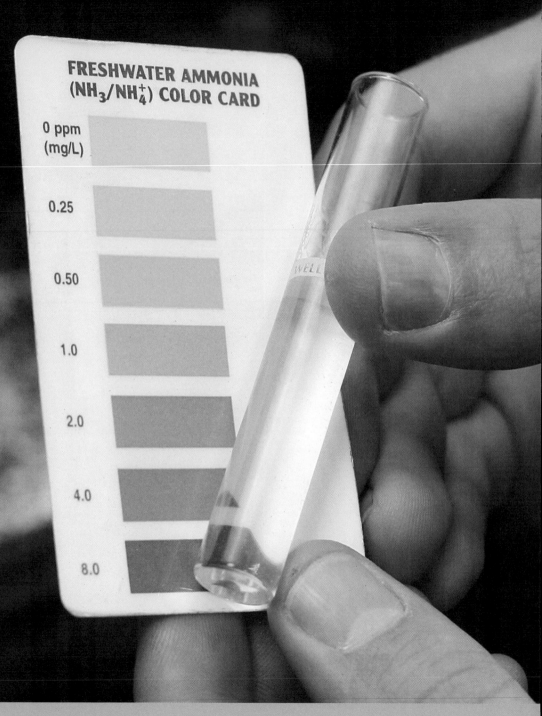

POWER ON

With dry hands (!) switch on the power supply feeding the power filter and heaterstat. You can leave the lights off for the time being as there's no plant or animal life in the tank to affect. You can also leave the hood off or open, but make sure the condensation trays are shut to keep dirt and dust out of the tank.

After a couple of hours check the temperature of the water with your thermometer. If you've opted for an in-tank thermometer rather than a stick-on-the-front digital version, just dip the thermometer in the tank (you can attach it by its suckers after planting; it's a lot easier!). Keep a record of the temperature changes in a notebook, along with a note about the state of the room – warm, cold, morning or afternoon, and the season. This record will be useful in the future as it will give you an idea of how quickly or slowly the water temperature is raised in the tank. Check the filter system is working and adjust the direction – remember it should be from the back diagonally across the tank – and the rate of flow as required.

Twenty-four hours should be enough time for any cloudiness in the water to be removed by the filtration system, but it's not long enough for those vital good bacteria to colonise the foam insert in the power filter. If we remember that these bacteria play a vital role in maintaining water quality, they need time to become established so they can do their work.

TESTING THE WATER

As the aquarium keeper, you are ultimately in control of the conditions inside the tank. Before anything (especially fish) is added to the new tank, the water must be tested using a simple testing kit. This will tell you that the filter is indeed working correctly and that water conditions are stable.

In a new tank you'll need to test for nitrites and ammonia at least twice a week in the first 6 or 7 weeks and then every 7 to 14 days you'll need to test the water to find the levels of nitrites, ammonia and pH to maintain its condition.

To ensure that results from your water test are entirely accurate, rinse the vial from the test kit in the aquarium water – not in tap water – so you don't get any false readings.

TESTING THE NITRITE AND NITRATE LEVELS MUST BE DONE TWICE A WEEK FOR THE FIRST 6-7 WEEKS OF A NEW TANKS RUNNING IN PERIOD, AND THEN EVERY 7-14 DAYS THEREAFTER TO MONITOR AND MAINTAIN SAFE LEVELS. AT THE SAME TIME, TEST FOR pH LEVELS.

Making a display

Now that the aquarium is up and running and the filter and heaterstat are working properly, the next step is to add some plants. You could, of course, take the easy option and chose artificial (plastic) plants: they are easy to care for, they look very convincing and you just clip pieces together to change the length of the stems and bunch the stems together to make a display. Plastic plants are quite good at hiding essential equipment in the tank, but they won't do a thing for removing those deadly nitrates from the water. If you use plastic plants in your aquarium then it is vital that you pay routine and very regular attention to the efficiency of your water filter and make those important water changes regularly.

The next section deals with aquatic plants: which to choose for your tank, how to buy them, how to plant, and how and what to feed them so they flourish in your aquarium and form part of the cycle of life in the biotope.

As well as their visual impact, aquatic plants provide a number of benefits to the aquarium: during the time that the tank is illuminated, aquatic plants reduce the amount of carbon dioxide dissolved in the water; they offer the fish areas of sanctuary for rest, shelter and shade; they can provide suitable spawning sites for breeding; and they make the habitat look much more natural. Many popular aquarium plants are rooted in the gravel substrate of the tank and draw their nutrients from the salts dissolved in the aquarium water, but there are other aquatic plants that float with their roots trailing in the water. While there are hundreds of plants available to choose from, some will flourish in a freshwater aquarium while others need more specialised conditions.

AQUARIUM STOCKISTS WILL HAVE A WIDE RANGE OF FURNISHINGS FOR THE TANK INCLUDING 'PLASTIC PLANTS'. ALTHOUGH REALISTIC LOOKING AND GOOD FOR DISGUISING HEATERSTATS AND FILTERS IN THE TANK, PLASTIC PLANTS WILL NOT WORK IN THE NITROGEN CYCLE TO REMOVE NITRATES AND NITRATES FROM THE WATER AND A WELL MAINTAINED FILTER WITH A GOOD COLONY OF BACTERIA IS VITAL.

planting an aquarium

your freshwater aquarium

THINK BEFORE YOU BUY

While the aquarium is running in and the filters and heaters are working to bring the water to its optimum conditions, the aquarist can spend some time researching plants: some aquatic plants require less light than others and there are plants of different heights, shapes and densities, as well as many shades of green to choose from. It's a good idea to avoid impulse buying and start with just a few specimen plants. You can always add more later and you may be able to propagate the plants you already have by taking cuttings once the plants are established. Always check the mature height and spread of the plants – how big they will grow – because you don't want plants that will outgrow your aquarium in a few months.

WHERE TO PLANT

If you made a plan of the aquarium with the hard furnishings such as rocks and wood sketched in, you could use this to help plan your planting scheme. Since you are creating an underwater scene that should look quite natural but pleasing to the eye, again consider the aquarium as your stage set: use some taller plants for the background and edges of the tank and smaller foreground plants that will not block your view but will still give the fish some cover and shade. You might also want to consider whether to include a single, distinctive, dazzling specimen plant to provide impact in the middle ground or just a few plants that will grow to just about mid-height of the tank. The important thing though is not to over-plant the tank – those fish have to swim somewhere! Plantings in groups of three, rather than a straight line of individual plants, looks very effective and more natural in the tank.

HOW MANY PLANTS

Because the aquarium will offer a stable environment, the aquatic plants in the tank will flourish, so a careful eye needs to be kept on them: regular submarine pruning will be needed to keep their height and spread in check. A useful rule of thumb for planting is to have one type of plant for every 10 cm (4 in) of front tank glass: if your aquarium is 60 cm (24 in) long, you have room for six plants.

THE TROPICAL FISH KEEPER IS ALSO THE KEEPER OF AQUATIC PLANTS AND THESE NEED TO BE MATCHED TO REPLICATE THE NATURAL HABITATS OF THE SPECIES KEPT IN THE TANK. SOME SPECIES ARE HERBIVOROUS AND REQUIRE PLANTS FOR THEIR FEED WHILE OTHERS REQUIRE PLANTS TO SWIM THROUGH AND IN WHICH TO REST OR HIDE IF THEY FEEL THREATENED. JUST AS IN ANY GARDEN, THE SUBMARINE PLANTS REQUIRE FEEDING AND PRUNING TO KEEP THEM HEALTHY.

Buying plants

Most aquatic suppliers will stock a range of tropical aquarium plants for you to choose from. The plants should be displayed in the tanks so you can see them clearly. In addition to the price, they should be labelled with their name, mature height and spread, and, in a good shop, with their best location in the tank – foreground, middle or background.

BUNCHED AND POTTED PLANTS

Aquatic plants are usually sold in two forms: in bunches or in little basket pots. The potted plants may be a little more expensive, but most of the time it's worth the extra money because these plants have strong established roots and are generally healthy. In each pot or basket there may be three or more pieces of protective rock wool, and each piece may have two or three plants. For planting, potted plants are removed from their outer pots and left with their roots covered in the rock wool. The base of the plant is planted just below the gravel substrate.

Examine each plant slowly and carefully and reject any that look sick: a healthy plant will have hole-free leaves and roots and small plantlets growing around the base of the pot. Avoid any plants that have damaged leaves or roots, are rotting or turning yellow – the last indicates a lack of nutrients and it may be too late to save these specimens so choose another healthy plant instead.

When you have selected your plants, the retailer should wrap them in individual polythene bags that are then filled with air and sealed to prevent the plants from being crushed or bruised in transit.

Bunched plants usually consist of a few individual plants tied together with a weight. Remove the weight and separate out the stems. Holding the stem of the plant gently near the base, wiggle a finger on the same hand into the substrate to make a little hole. Slide in the plant and then use your finger to rearrange the substrate around the base of the stem. In difficult to reach – or very deep tanks – you may need to use a planting stick for gently pushing in the plants roots. You can buy planting sticks but look for one where the reverse end can mount a razor blade so you can also use the stick as an algae scraper to remove growth from the glass walls of the tank (see 'Plants and Algae' p136).

PLANTING UP AN AQUARIUM MEANS ROLLING UP YOUR SLEEVES: WIGGLING A FINGER GENTLY INTO THE SUBSTRATE TO MAKE A PLANTING HOLE, POPPING THE PLANT IN THE HOLE, HOLDING IT IN PLACE AND THEN WIGGLING A SPARE FINGER AROUND TO BACK FILL THE HOLE MAY SOUND TRICKY, BUT IS ACTUALLY OFTEN EASIER THAN 'DISTANCE' PLANTING USING A PLANTING STICK. IN TIME, AND UNDER WELL MANAGED CONDITIONS, THE PLANTS WILL THRIVE AND FILL UP SPACE SO YOU MAY HAVE TO GO IN AND PRUNE THEM BACK A BIT.

your freshwater aquarium

Which plants?

Remember that the size and number of plants you choose for your aquarium will be informed by the size of your tank but you may like to consider a mix of stem plants, where the leaves are located so far apart that you can see the stem or stalk between them, and rosette plants, whose leaves are arranged in the shape of a rosette. Such a mix of plants would give pleasing contrasts in height and shape as well as colour.

As a general rule, aquatic plants with fine, feathery or red coloured leaves (which require greater levels of light) are a little more difficult to keep in an aquarium: too little light and they grow straggly or leggy; too much light and they will grow very quickly. Ask the plant supplier for advice with these types of plants: they will be able to suggest the perfect spots in your tank. There are many plants to choose from. The ones listed below are some of the more popular aquatic plants suitable for the tropical freshwater aquarium. Just as in a garden centre, aquatic plants have a Latin name: this is given alongside its common name, a description of the plant and some useful information, such as its height or location in the tank.

ROOTED PLANTS

Amazon sword plant (Echinodorus species) There are several types of plants that go by the name of Amazon sword plant: there are tall plants that make beautiful single-specimen plants, varieties with ruffled leaves and dwarf varieties. As their name suggests, the species is native to tropical South America: look out for *E. paniculatus*; *E. tennellus*; *E. major* (the ruffled sword plant) for use as a feature plant and *E. magdalenensis* (the dwarf Amazon sword plant) for use in foreground planting. The Amazon sword plant propagates itself by sending out long runners from the main plant on which new plantlets grow – a bit like the spider plant familiar as a houseplant. Push the base of the young plant into the substrate and let the new baby plant establish itself: alternatively, you could pass on or trade your new plant with a fellow tropical fish enthusiast.

Anacharis or elodea (*Elodea densa*) Anacharis is probably the very first plant a novice tropical freshwater aquarium keeper will buy: it's popular because it demands very little from its surroundings and because the amount of light will determine the colour of the leaves. These vary from really dark green to pale lime green. Anacharis is ideal for a space at the rear of the tank: keep an eye on it because it grows rapidly and needs to be pruned regularly. In the wild it can grow up to 4 m (13 ft) tall and if it grows too tall in the tank, the bottom part of the stem will go bald!

YOUR AQUARIUM STOCKIST SHOULD HAVE A RANGE OF PLANTS CLEARLY LABELLED WITH THEIR NAMES. DON'T BE AFRAID TO ASK FOR ADVICE ABOUT PLANTS AND ALWAYS TELL THE STOCKIST WHAT SIZE OF TANK YOU HAVE AND WHAT TYPE OF FISH YOU PLAN ON KEEPING.

Bacopa (*Bacopa caroliniana*) This bacopa species grows well (especially in hard water) and is a good plant for the back or mid zone of the tank. It has fleshy green stalks with shield-shaped leaves that are arranged in pairs on either side of the stem. Before planting, remove the lowest pair of leaves and take care not to bruise the fleshy stem.

Cabomba or standard green cabomba (*Cabomba caroliniana*) This plant is a native of North America and is good for providing spawning areas. It roots easily but does need clean water otherwise sediment will block up the gorgeous whorls of leaves that grow to about 3.75 cm (1.5 in) across. Cabomba also likes pretty still water: turbulence will break up its delicate leaves, so plant it in a quiet but well-lit spot where it will thrive.

Java fern (*Microsorium pteroptus*) Found in the wild in India and the Far East, the Java fern has long, yet quite broad, leaves with attractive dark spots, and grows up to 30 cm (12 in). Its Latin species name *pteroptus* means 'grows on rocks': the rootstock of Java fern clings to rocks and wood – although it can take some months before the plant is fully established – and the plant produces young plants that form on the leaves. It's an attractive plant that does well in subdued light conditions: in bright light the leaves can develop clear patches that can later turn brown.

Cryptocoryne There are a few species of the Cryptocoryne genus native to Southeast Asia that are popular in tropical freshwater aquaria: *C. ciliata* grows to about 50 cm (20 in) tall so is ideal for deep aquaria. Shorter but no less attractive alternatives are *C. willisii* from Sri Lanka, which grows up to 20 cm (8 in) tall (the stems are narrow at the base and broaden out at the ends to form long leaves); *C. wendtii* (also from Sri Lanka), which varies in size from 10–30 cm (4–12 in) and in leaf colour from specimen to specimen (with the top and bottom sides of the leaves a different colour); and *C. nevillii*, which grows to a height between 13–20 cm (5–8 in) high.

Water wisteria (Hygrophilia)
The water wisteria is native to the Far East. There are a variety of wisterias to choose from, with the most popular being easy-rooting *Hygrophilia difformis* (also known as *Synnema triflorum*) with its light green leaves and spread of up to 10 cm (4 in). It's a good plant for backgrounds but the shape will vary depending on the lighting conditions: poor light will make it grow long and lanky, good light will make it bushy. Other types of wisteria include *H. polysperma*, which has 2.5–5 cm (1–2 in) long leaves placed alternatively on the stem. This is a fast-growing bushy wisteria, so it makes a good tank filler and cuttings taken from it root very easily. *H. salicifolia* is the willow leaf hygrophilia and, as its name implies, its leaves are

your freshwater aquarium

long, thin and dangly like a willow and look very attractive in gently undulating water.

Eelgrass (*Vallisneria natans*) Widespread throughout the tropics, eelgrass is a favourite background plant. It can grow up to 90 cm (36 in) tall but the twisted variety (*V. tortifolia*) with its gorgeous corkscrewing leaves doesn't tend to grow quite as tall and so is ideally suited to the smaller aquarium. Don't be misled by the variety name of *Vallisnera spiralis*: this is in fact a straight-growing eelgrass whose flower spike alone is spiralled.

Ludwigia (Ludwigia species) There are a number of varieties of ludwigia: *L. mullertii* has lovely red leaves but, remember, coloured leaves require more light than green-leafed plants. For the green-leafed ludwigia, try *L. repens* or *L. palutris*. All are versatile plants that, once established, will grow prolifically, so keep them well under control with regular pruning – and you can use the cuttings to plant in the tank to create new plants.

These are just a few 'planted' plants: take your time and find out more about the species available and what they require in terms of hard or soft, acid or alkaline water.

FLOATING PLANTS

Not all aquatic plants have roots planted in the substrate: some float on the surface water in the aquarium. Some aquarium keepers regard floating plants as nuisances: the surface of the water is where the exchange of gasses takes place and if the surface is covered by floating plants, the exchange won't take place. Floating plants – in small quantities – do nonetheless offer shade for fishes from the almost non-stop glare of the lights in the aquarium hood. These plants also offer sanctuary to young fry who can seek safety in their dangling root systems, and many of the gourami species of fish utilise fragments of this plant material in the construction of their bubble nests, as the root fibres help stop the bubble nest from disintegrating. Floating plants range in size from the very small to the quite enormous but the most popular for the average aquarium include:

Crystalwort (*Riccia fluitans*) Distributed worldwide in tropical waters, Crystalwort is a multi-branched floating plant that forms dense mats. Light requirements are not critical to its growth and it provides nice shade and refuge for fry.

Fairy Moss (*Azolla caroliniana*) Native to the tropical waters of North America, Fairy Moss has leaves up to about 1.25 cm (1/2 in) long and, depending on the light, some may be reddish in colour.

Indian Fern (*Ceratopsis thalictroides*) is an excellent 'compromise': it's a floating plant that does equally well if planted in the substrate, so you can change your mind or use it to provide floating refuge for fry when needed.

AS WITH GARDENING ON LAND, SOME PLANTS THRIVE, OTHERS WITHER AWAY. GIVE YOUR 'WATERSCAPE' AND THE PLANTS TIME TO SETTLE IN: REMOVE DEAD AND DYING PLANTS AND REPLACE WITH STRONG HEALTHY ONES. DON'T OVER-PLANT BUT LEAVE PLENTY OF SPACE FOR THEM TO FILL OUT- AND FOR THE FISH WHO WILL NEED TO SWIM THROUGH AND BETWEEN THEM.

Planting techniques

Once you have decided on your plants and their location in the tank, you need to plant them. This can be a bit fiddly and it's best done using just one hand. Roll your sleeves up or, better still, take off your shirt – there's no way it won't get wet!

As mentioned earlier, many plants are sold in little pots or baskets, so the first step is to remove the outer basket or pot by carefully cutting the plastic and peeling it away. This will reveal the rock wool growing medium without damaging the plant's roots.

Now, very gently, remove as much of the rock wool growing medium from around the roots as you can, taking care not to damage the roots. If the roots are very long, trim them so you can 'fan' them out when you come to plant them in the substrate.

Remove any damaged leaves and check the leaves over for snails or their eggs: these will appear as blobs of jelly on the leaves. Gently rub them off: you don't want them growing in your aquarium.

Next, look at the plant and rotate it to see if it has a 'good' or 'better' side: this is the side you want facing outwards in the tank. Hold the base of the plant gently in a cradle of fingers and position it on the spot where you want to plant it. With one finger, wiggle the substrate to make a planting hole and pop the plant in. Backfill with the gravel substrate to hold the plant in place.

If the plants are bought loose in bundles, untie the lead weight from the bundle and separate out each plant. Hold them gently at the base of the stalk and plant as you would the 'potted' versions – by wiggling them into a hole in the substrate and backfilling afterwards. You may also want to add an extra 'anchor' by placing a small pebble at the base of the plant.

MANY PLANTS ARE SOLD IN BUNDLES, TIED TOGETHER, OR IN LITTLE POTS OR BASKETS WHICH HAVE TO BE REMOVED. CAREFULLY CUT THE PLASTIC BASKET OR POT AWAY AND YOU WILL FIND THE ROOTS OF THE PLANTS WRAPPED IN ROCK WOOL, A GROWING MEDIUM. THIS IS VERY GENTLY PRISED AWAY FROM THE PLANT ROOTS: BE CAREFUL NOT TO DAMAGE THE ROOTS THOUGH.

ATTACHING A PLANT TO WOOD

Some plants, like the Java fern, prefer to grow on a piece of wood. Planting these attractive plants is very easy to do: you'll need a piece of cleaned and prepared wood (see Aquascaping on page 109), some dark nylon thread, a pair of sharp scissors and, naturally, a healthy Java fern. This plant grows from a rhizome: lay this on top of your piece of wood and, with a good long length of nylon thread, wind the thread over the rhizome – between the leaves of the plant – and attach it to the wood. Take care that you don't pull the thread too tightly or you can cut into the rhizome or damage the base of the leaves. Securely tie the thread and then cut off any dangling ends. The plant is now ready for the tank. It may take several months for the plant to establish itself completely, but once established, the fine roots will spread out and take hold of the wood.

FEEDING PLANTS

The plants in the aquarium get a large proportion of the food they need from the waste products produced by the fish, but a regular feed with plant fertiliser in liquid or tablet form will give them an extra boost. Read the instructions very carefully: remember to refer to your new volume measurement of water that takes account of the water displaced by the equipment and furnishings (not the original tank capacity) in order to make the correct feed solution. Tablet fertilisers can be placed close to the plant roots, buried in the substrate.

PROPAGATING PLANTS BY CUTTINGS

Many cuttings taken from popular aquarium plants are harvested from the wild in tropical regions during the dry season. With less water around, the plants develop woody stems and may even flower. Furthermore, their leaf shapes in dry form may be very different to the shapes they take on under water. When you shop for plants, you can tell easily if a plant has been grown in or out of water: a plant grown out of water will not 'flop over' when you hold it at the base of the stem, while a plant grown in water will 'flop' because the water pressure would normally be holding it upright. You can use the woody cuttings to plant up and make new strong plants: put them in a spare tank of water and wait for the leaves to die off, removing them one by one as they die. After a while, shoots should appear from some of the leaf joints: when this happens, cut off the underwater growths and plant them in the substrate as you would a 'new' plant. With luck they will take root and grow and you'll have brand new plants to go in your aquarium – or trade with a fellow enthusiast.

PLANTS ANCHORED TO PIECES OF WOOD MAKE FOR AN ATTRACTIVE AQUASCAPE AND SOME PLANTS LIKE THE JAVA FERN GROW ON WOOD NATURALLY. THE RHIZOME ROOT OF SUCH PLANTS CAN BE SECURED TO A PIECE OF WOOD BY SOME NYLON THREAD.

Plants and algae

The moment the conditions are right for growth, algae will appear in your aquarium. It's important to understand and find out the source of algae growth: algae can occur when new light is added to the tank, when there is surplus food in the water, when the water has not been changed for a long time or when you have introduced plants (many will have traces of algae on them when you buy them). It's a good idea to keep a logbook noting the occurrence of algae and recording all the important details such as when new lights were installed, and when new plants and fish were introduced. This way you can see not only when something went 'wrong' but what may have caused the problem. The aquarium keeper also needs to become familiar with the different types of algae that can appear in the tank and how to deal with it.

Thread algae

Thread algae looks a bit like 'mini seaweed' and is the type of algae the novice will often find in a newly started aquarium. It can occur particularly if your tap water has a lot of calcium in it: the water ends up in the tank and the calcium provides nutrients to the algae. Thread algae is relatively harmless and it can even be useful because it does remove many of the unnecessary nutrients in the tank. If you don't want thread algae spoiling your display, you must ensure that your water is correctly treated and is kept low in nutrients.

Beard algae

Beard algae has green-black threads, which can be quite long and often hang off the edges of leaves. It's an algae you don't want in your tank: it's a form of 'red algae' and is normally introduced to the tank on a plant. If you spot this on plant leaves, it's best to remove the plant completely from the tank and dispose of it.

Fuzz algae

Fuzz algae looks a lot like beard algae and, if it is introduced into your tank on a new plant, it will pretty soon overgrow it! The best way to deal with this algae is to introduce fish species that eat it: the Mexican highland carp loves fuzz algae (but these fish need feeding well, otherwise they'll eat up all your plants too!). Many aquarium clubs have a library – like loan system and lend these fish to owners to deal with the problem – another good reason for joining a local club!

HEALTHY FISH ARE HAPPY FISH: ROUTINE AND RIGOROUS ATTENTION TO TANK MAINTENANCE AND HYGIENE WILL HELP FISH- AND PLANTS- TO THRIVE.

Black brush algae

Black brush algae, despite its name, is a form of 'red algae' and varies in colour from black to a spinach green, with a red layer hidden underneath. This algae is difficult to remove and you must sacrifice the plant to remove it.

Brown and green algae

Brown algae is usually very harmless: it can be found all over the tank, on rocks, on equipment, on the glass walls – everywhere. In the event of brown algae, the message is to be economical with the food and make sure the water composition is correct. You can remove brown algae with an algae scraper, or you can leave it where it is: once you have reduced the amount of food the brown algae generally disappears! Brown algae may also appear when an aquarium is being prepared and is newly planted: this will usually disappear once the aquarium has been run in – a reason why no fish are introduced at the planting stage! Green algae in your aquarium can't do much damage either: it's often a sign that your water quality is very good! It's still good to remove it from the tank, though, because the green algae are 'eating' the same nutrients as your plants. Green algae have greenish threads, often 'woven' together, and you can remove it from the water with your hand. If you're not keen on this method, then dip a cotton wool bud into the algae and 'roll it up' to remove it!

Blue algae

This slimy form of algae needs to be removed from your tank. Despite its name, blue algae doesn't always appear blue: it can be blue-green or even black-brown, but it gets everywhere in the tank. It normally starts at the bottom of the tank and covers the whole surface in a stinking, slimy layer: you'll know it's blue algae by the hideous smell! To remove it, you can suck it out with a pipe from your aquarium supplier. If you can't do this, then there are other ways of dealing with it: again, keep a good, accurate logbook so that you can find the cause of the algae occurrence and avoid it in the future. Blue algae need light to survive, so switch off the light in the aquarium for three days and cover the whole tank in a dark blanket – effectively blocking out all light. After that time, the algae will be dead and you can scoop it out with a bucket. Slowly increase the light levels little by little – every day a little longer. This way your aquarium will get going again gently: any plants that were in the tank during the 'three-day total eclipse' will look a bit pale and weedy but they usually survive and recover. Any that don't, take out and replace as needed.

FOR ALGAE TO GROW, CONDITIONS MUST BE RIGHT: IT CAN OCCUR WHEN A NEW LIGHT SOURCE IS ADDED TO THE TANK, WHEN THERE IS A SURPLUS OF FOOD IN THE TANK, WHEN NEW PLANTS HAVE BEEN INTRODUCED- OR WHEN THERE ARE TOO MANY PLANTS FOR THE SIZE OF TANK- AND WHEN THE TANKS' WATER HAS NOT BEEN ROUTINELY CHANGED.

MORE WINNING WAYS WITH ALGAE!

One of the best ways of avoiding algae growth in your aquarium is to avoid siting it in bright sunlight. The location of your tank should have taken this into consideration, but it's not always possible to see how the light falls through a window at different times of the year. It may be that you now have to move the tank to a new spot! Bright light causes the plants in the aquarium to use too many nutrients and a deficiency will follow. Algae too, as we mentioned, can be introduced into the tank by new plants: this is why it's important to examine each prospective purchase slowly and carefully. If you are in doubt about the suitability of a new plant, ask for advice, or take an experienced aquarist with you. If the plants in your tank are growing well, then there is little room for the algae – the competition is too much for them. Algae may grow, however, if you over-feed the plants (misnomer because the plants are effectively 'wasting' the food they don't need and so the algae feed on it instead): feed plants only while they are 'doing well' and stop feeding if algae starts to be a problem.

Algae flourish when the water in the tank hasn't been changed in time: depending on the size of your tank, it's a good idea to change about 1/5 of the water each week. Don't replace all of the water unless you are planning to start the tank again from scratch.

Since algae grows on all surfaces, it will also grow on the inside walls of the tank. You can remove this using your planting stick with the handy razor blade holder at the other end. Use the razor blade to scrape the algae off the glass. Alternatively, invest in an algae magnet – a device that is in fact two strong magnets: one sits inside the tank, the other 'magnetically held' on the outside. Without even getting your hands wet (in theory at least), you can 'clean the windows' on the inside of the tank of algae. You will, however, have to take the magnet out at some stage to clean it – and remember not to pull the outside magnet away from the glass or the inner magnet will drop to the bottom of the tank. Whichever method you use, algae cleaning will become part of your routine aquarium maintenance.

ALGAE GROWS ON ALL SURFACES INCLUDING SUBSTRATES AND ON THE TANK GLASS. THERE ARE MANY TYPES OF ALGAE BUT THE MOST COMMON ARE BROWN AND GREEN ALGAE WHICH CAN BE REMOVED BY 'FISHING' IT OUT WITH YOUR HAND OR BY SCRAPING IT FROM THE TANK WALLS WITH AN ALGAE SCRAPER.

Time for the fish

Getting the plants established and running in the aquarium takes around 7–10 days. This gives you time to make any changes to the landscaping, check that there are no leaks, all the equipment is running properly, the temperature and quality of the water are at the correct levels, the filter has had time to remove any pollutants, and you have cleaned up any algae you may inadvertently have introduced at the planting stage. During this period, the ammonia and nitrite levels in the water will rise and they must drop back to zero before fish are introduced.

Once all the conditions are right and stable, the first fish can at last be introduced. At this stage, the filter will have to start cleaning up the waste produced by the fish: this process takes time as the bacteria in the foam inserts in the filter need to colonise so they can do their work. The delay can cause dangerous fluctuations in the water quality so the tank must be monitored very regularly. You could, of course, wait a few more weeks before adding the fish: some aquarists advocate adding special bacterial products to the tank for up to a month before introducing any fish. While the idea of another month-long 'fishless cycle' might not appeal, the benefits include a 'mature' bacteria colony in the filter medium and a reduced number of problems normally associated with new aquaria.

The next section deals with selecting fish for the tropical freshwater aquarium. You will discover:
- How to choose healthy fish
- How many to buy for your size tank
- What species to buy
- What size fish to buy
- Whether the fish like to be alone, in pairs, in trios or in schools
- Where they like to be in the tank
- Which species will live happily in a 'community tank' with others.

LIKE FISH, PLANTS ALSO NEED TO BE FED. BUT TOO MUCH PLANT FOOD CAN CAUSE ALGAE GROWTH SO MAKE SURE YOU READ AND FOLLOW THE DOSAGE INSTRUCTIONS GIVEN BY THE MANUFACTURER.

choosing fish

Now that the aquarium is furnished, aquascaped and planted and has been run in for at least 10 days to filter and stabilise the water (ideally for longer if you can be patient – to ensure the tank is completely mature and the plants have successfully rooted and are established), you can start to think about adding some fish. It's important to consider the number, size, species and habits of the fish well in advance of introducing them to their new environment: start with just a few fish and build up the numbers over a period of six to eight weeks – or even longer.

TAKE YOUR TIME

Choosing the right fish for your aquarium takes time, thought and patience: you want the right fish for your tank's environment and you want them to be healthy. It's easy to be seduced by the gorgeous colours and fantastic shapes of fish on offer but you must check the specific requirements for each species – water conditions, temperature and suitability of tank mates before you buy.

Remember, too, that many of these fish will have already travelled halfway around the world to reach your supplier: they've probably got settled into their tank and now face another upsetting relocation. The more stress-free you can make the transition for them, the better for the fish. A stressed fish is more likely to contract a disease than a relaxed one, so it's important to get them off to a happy start. Don't rush the introduction of fish: the more perfect the environment, the happier and healthier they will be.

THE SIAMESE FIGHTING FISH (BETTA SPLENDENS) IS A POPULAR AQUARIUM FISH AND HAS BEEN BRED IN A GREAT RANGE OF COLOURS FROM BLACKS AND BLUES TO GREEN AND RED. SOME ALSO HAVE ELABORATE FIN SHAPES THAT WHEN EXPANDED, THE SHAPE OF THE FISH WHEN SEEN FROM SIDEWAYS ON IS ALMOST A COMPLETE CIRCLE. AGGRESSIVE TOWARDS OTHER MALES OF THE SPECIES, THE SIAMESE FIGHTING FISH IS GENERALLY VERY PEACEFULLY IN-CLINED TO OTHER FISH- PROVIDED THEY ARE LARGE ENOUGH NOT TO BE RE-GARDED AS FOOD!

THE TROPICAL COMMUNITY AQUARIUM

When you visit the tropical aquarium shop you will be faced with a huge variety of tropical freshwater fish of all shapes, colours and sizes. Most of the fish that are kept successfully in aquariums belong to a small number of large groups, each with distinct characteristics. The term 'community fish' is used to describes species that will live happily with other peaceful fish – but use this term with caution, as not all community fish will live without causing some disruption. Some fish may nip at long-finned fish causing them distress, so the nippers are best in a community of short-finned fish. Some fish enjoy the quiet life and get stressed if a boisterous or a very large neighbour moves in – even though both might be called community fish. What you definitely don't want is a community at war, so predatory species must be excluded unless you want your stock to be eaten up! Likewise, if you have too many vegetarian fish in your tank, you can wave goodbye to your plants! And if you are planning on breeding fish, bear in mind that some species of live-bearing fish will interbreed with the same species regardless of colour pattern, so, if you want 'pure strains' of live bearers, don't mix the colours of fish in your tank! Don't forget too that some fish may well be nocturnal in their habits, so you won't see them swimming around when the tank is illuminated to reproduce daylight.

Understanding the different species of fish that will live happily together in the aquarium is the first step in creating a healthy community and a beautiful display: some of the smaller species such as barbs, tetras, danios and rasboras are fish that live in schools and should be kept in groups of at least four to six. Other fish, such as dwarf gourami, are happiest when they are in a pair or a trio, while a male Siamese fighting fish is best kept on his own so he doesn't fight other males. Furthermore, some male fish are pretty ardent suitors and it's best to buy a trio of one male and two females so that one single female is not constantly harassed. Remember, too, that different species of fish have different habits, diets and habitats so you must be prepared to provide these for all the species in your tank: for example if you want to keep a catfish in your community tank, the substrate will need to have plenty of soft sandy areas. Before you add any new fish to the community, make sure you do your homework first and ensure their new home is perfect.

THE DWARF GOURAMI (COLISA LALIA) MAY BE THE SMALLEST OF THE
GOURAMI BUT IS ONE OF THE MOST ATTRACTIVE WITH ITS RED GROUND AND
DOUBLE-STRIPED FLANKS OF BRIGHT PALE BLUE AND GREEN AND BRIGHT RED
TAIL FIN (AND TIPS OF THE ANAL AND PELVIC FINS). THESE LITTLE FISH LOVE
'SUNSHINE', ARE HAPPY IN A COMMUNITY TANK WITH FISH THE SAME SIZE
AND THRIVE IN TANKS WHERE THERE IS ALGAE FOR THEM TO FEED ON- SAVING
YOU THE JOB OF CLEANING IT OUT!

WHERE DO FISH SWIM?

This may sound like an odd question, given that the answer is 'in water', but in fact, the true answer is a little more complicated. It's more a question of 'where do the different fish like to swim the most'?

Many fish have preferred habitats. Some like the bottom levels of water near the riverbed or lakebed, so in the aquarium, the bottom layer of the tank and its waters become the 'home from home' for the foraging fish such as catfish and loach – remember their mouths are turned down to help them root around in the substrate for food. The middle layer of water in the aquarium, which is the largest zone in the tank, is the favoured habitat for the schooling fish such as the barbs and tetras – their mouths are central on their heads for feeding 'straight on'– while the top 5cm (2 in) of water is the home for those species of fish, like gouramis, with upturned mouths which like to swim and feed at the water's surface. Understanding these zone preferences means you can populate the aquarium with a variety of species that will live happily in a community without 'getting on each other's nerves'.

SIZE AND NUMBER OF FISH

Don't overpopulate your aquarium: it's important that stock levels are in keeping with the size of your tank. When you calculate the number of fish your tank can accommodate, don't forget to factor in their mature size (see Choosing a Tank, page 68–77). Always double-check with the aquarium dealer for peace of mind. Each fish needs about 3 litres (6 pt) of water: this is not just for swimming space, but to hold the necessary amount of oxygen dissolved in the water to sustain the fish's life. Too many fish means competition for oxygen and it also means additional waste products that cannot be processed effectively, so the tank becomes polluted and toxic. As you get more experienced and more knowledgeable, you will be able to make more informed decisions on your own.

FOUND EXCLUSIVELY IN THE WILD ONLY IN THE 'OLD WORLD' AND DIVISIBLE INTO ASIATIC AND AFRICAN SPECIES, BARBS HAVE ALWAYS BEEN FAVOURITES WITH AQUARISTS: ACTIVE, YET PEACEFUL FISH, THEY ARE BRIGHTLY AND BEAUTIFULLY COLOURED. BARBS ARE SOME OF THE EASIEST FISH TO KEEP AND THE SMALLER SPECIES LIVE FOR TWO TO THREE YEARS: THEY ARE HAPPY IN BOTH HARD AND SOFT WATER BUT DO PREFER VERY WELL- FILTERED WATER AND AS SHOAL FISH, ENJOY THE COMPANY OF OTHERS OF THEIR OWN SPECIES.

your freshwater aquarium

WHAT TO LOOK FOR

When the time comes to make your first selection of fish for your aquarium there are a few tips to help you choose the best and healthiest specimens. Compare stocks held by different suppliers and note any differences in condition, quality and price. Look to see if the selling tanks are clean and well maintained, with no dead fish in them. The tanks should be labelled, detailing the fish in them, price, potential size, any special dietary requirements and compatibility with other fish. A reputable dealer will have done this – and more – to ensure his stock is the best it can be, to encourage and promote interest and enthusiasm in keeping fish and, of course, maintain his reputation.

Take your time examining the fish in the tanks: most freshwater fish swim with their dorsal fin erect: avoid any fish with a folded down dorsal fin as this can be a sign of illness. The fish's body should be 'well filled': hollow bellies and skinny, emaciated bodies don't always mean the fish need a good meal but can be a symptom of disease. The colours of the fish should be bright and clear and any colour patterns should be clearly defined: avoid specimens with smudging of one colour into the next. Look also at the way the fish is swimming: it should be effortless and without a 'wobble', and it should be able to remain at any depth in the water without sinking to the bottom or floating to the surface. Avoid any fish with missing fins or other obvious defects, such as a misshapen body. Look to see what the other fish of the same species are doing: any individual who is acting strangely may be sick, so choose a specimen that is active and responsive – although bear in mind that some species are naturally quiet and retiring. Spend a good deal of time observing the fish: this will help you recognise the ones with the 'right' behaviour and best health and help you avoid taking home sick or injured specimens that might not survive the stress of being moved.

You'll want to populate the tank with both male and female fish. It's often quite easy to tell which are which: male live-bearing species have that telltale differently shaped anal fin, while in egg-laying species, as a general rule, the males are usually slimmer than the female, but more brightly coloured and often with more pronounced fins.

THE CLOWN LOACH (BOTIA MACARANTHUS), LIKE ALL LOACHES IS A QUIET, RATHER TIMID FISH THAT THRIVES WHEN TWO OR THREE ARE KEPT TOGETHER AND THERE ARE PLENTY OF STONE-AND-ROCK ARCHES FOR THEM TO HIDE UNDER. GROWING TO ABOUT 10CMS (4 INCHES), THE BRILLIANTLY ORANGE-RED COLOURED CLOWN LOACH HAS THREE VERTICAL DARK BROWN BARS- ONE THROUGH THEY EYE- BROWN DORSAL AND ANAL FINS AND OTHER FINS OF BRIGHT RED.

GETTING THEM HOME

Fish get stressed very easily when they are disturbed, and being netted out of a dealer's tank is naturally going to be upsetting for them. A reputable dealer will make sure that the packaging for your fish is suitable and comfortable: most are transported in plastic bags and, ideally, the bottom corners should be taped up so small fish don't get stuck in the pointy nook in the corners of the bag. There should be a small amount of water in the bag and a large amount of air, and the plastic bag should be inserted into a second, dark outer bag, because travelling in the dark is less stressful for the fish – they will think it's night and adjust their bodies to slow down and rest.

If you are travelling for more than half an hour between the dealer and home, tell the supplier. A reputable dealer will ensure that the plastic bag is further wrapped in newspaper or even set into an insulated box so the temperature of the transport water remains as constant as possible and the fish don't get chilled.

Acclimatising the fish

The next important stage in introducing the fish to the aquarium is to acclimatise them: any sudden changes in air or water temperature will stress them even further. Turn off all the aquarium lights and any bright lights in the room, to keep the lighting levels low so the fish aren't upset after being in the dark for a while. Take the outer wrapping off the plastic bag containing the fish. If your journey home has been short – around half an hour – then float the unopened plastic bag in the aquarium to bring the water in the bag to the same temperature as that in the aquarium. This normally takes about half an hour or so. If the fish have had a longer trip home, then carefully open the bag to provide some new fresh air. Carefully roll down the sides of the bag and hook it over the corner of the tank so it is held in place while the water temperatures equalise.

FISH TAKEN FROM A STORE'S TANK SHOULD BE TRANSPORTED IN A PLASTIC BAG JUST UNDER HALF FILLED WITH WATER FROM THE TANK IN WHICH THE FISH HAS BEEN KEPT. IDEALLY, THE BOTTOM EDGES OF THE BAG SHOULD BE TAPED UP SO VERY SMALL SPECIMENS DON'T GET TRAPPED IN THE CORNERS. A REPUTABLE DEALER WILL THEN INSERT THE BAG INTO A DARKER, OUTER BAG AS TRAVELLING IN THE DARK IS LESS STRESSFUL FOR THE FISH.

RELEASING THE FISH

Once the water in the bag has warmed up to the tank water's level, you can release the fish. Do this gently: don't just tip the fish into the tank (how would you like to be thrown into a swimming pool when you're still not wide awake!). Instead, gently turn the bag onto its side and hold the top open with one hand while you very slowly up-end the bag to encourage the fish to swim out into their new home.

As soon as the fish are in the tank, put the condensation tray back in place, replace the hood – taking care not to bang it and frighten the fish. Leave the aquarium lights off for another half an hour or so, then gradually, if possible, switch on the lights in the room (or open the blinds or curtains a bit) before you switch on the aquarium lights. The fish will naturally have taken cover in the plants and it will be a few minutes before they come out and start to explore their new surroundings. Leave the fish alone: don't feed them or disturb them for the next 24 hours. And remember to switch off the aquarium lights to give them their 10 hours or so of night-time rest. At this stage the fishes' colours won't be as bright as they were when you saw them in the dealer's tanks: this is normal because they are not sure about their new surroundings and are finding their way around. As soon as they have acclimatised to the tank and its features, their colours will improve, but this may take some days or even weeks. This is why the fish are introduced slowly and gradually to the tank, giving each of the new arrivals time to settle in and recover from their journey. Keep a check on the water temperature – by now this should be second nature to you – and remember that a fluctuation of one or two degrees is quite normal. Check the total number of fish every day over the next few weeks: if one's missing it may have not survived the stressful changes and its body must be found and removed from the tank, otherwise it will rot and pollute the water.

Tip: Introduce fish slowly and gradually to the new aquarium to give them a chance to recover from the stress of their journey and to allow them to become familiar with their new surroundings. Wait a few weeks until the water conditions have stabilised before introducing any new fish, and make sure you know exactly what conditions (habitat, temperature, water conditions, diet) are required for them to live happily.

FISH BROUGHT FROM A SUPPLIER SHOULD NOT BE 'TIPPED' INTO THEIR NEW TANK: THE WATER IN THEIR TRANSPORT BAG NEEDS TO BE BROUGHT UP TO THE SAME TEMPERATURE AS THE WATER IN THEIR NEW HOME. ONCE THIS HAS HAPPENED THE FISH CAN BE GENTLY ENCOURAGED TO SWIM OUT OF THE BAG AND EXPLORE THEIR NEW ENVIRONMENT.

STABILISING THE NEW ARRIVALS

In the weeks following the introduction of the first fish you need to check the filtration system is working properly and test for ammonia and nitrite levels: remember the good bacteria need to colonise the filter medium foam in order to do their work, so introducing the next batch of arrivals to the tank must wait until the colony has built up sufficiently to cope with an increase in numbers. In the meantime, you can always research more about the other fish you want to keep in your community tank.

Once the water test results are acceptable – it may take a few weeks – you can introduce some more fish, following the same routine as before. Check the total number of fish every time you buy and introduce new ones, just in case there have been any losses – or indeed new arrivals. The first fish in your tank will have marked out their territory and any newcomers who stray into their patch may cause some upset. When you introduce new fish, move around some of the rocks to dismantle the established territorial boundaries. Now all the fish will have to negotiate the new space.

ALWAYS TAKE YOUR TIME TO INTRODUCE NEW FISH INTO YOUR AQUARIUM AND CHECK ALL IS WORKING WELL BEFORE PLACING THE NEW ARRIVALS.

Popular fish for the community tank

Many of the fish described below are among the most popular species for the tropical freshwater aquarium and are ideal for the novice as they will live happily together – but they should not be introduced at the same time. Slowly build up the community and make sure they have enough room to thrive.

It was the Swedish naturalist Carl Linnaeus who introduced the binominal system of nomenclature – giving two names – to every living being, whether plant or animal. The first Latin name denotes the genus to which the fish belongs, while the second Latin name designates the species within the genus. So, like plants, fish have both a Latin scientific name and a common name. However, sometimes there are several common names, so it's a good idea to keep a list of the scientific names of your fish in your logbook so you can double-check that the species are compatible for community living. For example, the fish now known commonly as the cardinal tetra has a Latin name of *Paracheirodon axelrodi* – but it wasn't always so: at one time this tetra was named *Cheirodon alexrodi*. As more detailed knowledge is gained about the different fish, sometimes scientists realise that they have been placed in the incorrect genus and have to be renamed to reflect the newfound knowledge.

Since the Latin names can be a bit confusing, here we will be using the common name first and giving the Latin name afterwards. As you become experienced in looking after your aquarium, you will soon become very familiar with the scientific names.

DIFFERENT SPECIES OF FISH HAVE DIFFERENT HABITS AND HABITATS: SOME SPECIES LIKE TO OCCUPY THE BOTTOM REACHES OF WATER CLOSE TO THE SEA OR RIVER BED, WHILE OTHERS OCCUPY THE TOP THIRD OF THE WATER, CLOSE TO THE SURFACE. OCCUPYING THESE DIFFERENT 'ZONES' ALLOWS FOR DIFFERENT SPECIES TO LIVE SIDE BY SIDE- OR MORE ACCURATELY 'ON TOP OF EACH OTHER'- QUITE HAPPILY IN A COMMUNITY TANK.

THE CYPRINIDAE FAMILY

The Cyprinidae – or carp – family of fish includes around 1,250 species distributed in the wild across Europe, Africa, Asia, North and South America. In the tropical freshwater aquarium, among the most popular members of the Cyrpinidae family are the barbs. They get their name from the short, thread-like beards or 'barbels' (in Latin *barba* means 'beard') that have many touch organs to the left and right of their mouths (and sometimes on their lips too). Barbs have the classic streamlined fish shape that indicates they like to school in the mid-water zone of the aquarium. Most barbs are ideal for the novice to keep: they are easy to feed and they live on small aquatic insects, crustaceans and plant matter.

Also members of the Cyprinidae family are the rasboras, minnows and danios. These, too, are all fast-swimming schooling fish and, like barbs, are generally peaceable, and therefore very well suited to life in a community tank. They are also inexpensive and very hardy and should be the number one choice for the novice aquarist, and the first fish in a new tank. Another bonus is that in this group of fish, the zebra danio and the white cloud mountain minnow are among the easiest aquarium fish to breed.

Their lovely colours and great agility mean that this family of fish really enliven an aquarium, but it's a good idea to keep the smaller species separate from the larger species or the 'little ones' will suffer. Because these fish love to swim and dart in schools, the tank must be big enough to allow them to move freely. There should be plenty of planting around the sides of the tank for them to escape into, and because they are sensitive to pH levels above 7.5, ideally the pH level in the aquarium for these fish should be 6.5.

BARBS ARE ONE OF THE MOST POPULAR MEMBERS OF THE CYPRINIDAE FAMILY. THEY ARE IDEAL FOR 'NEW' FISH OWNERS, AS THEY ARE EASY TO CARE FOR AND PRETTY TO LOOK AT.

Popular Cyprinidae for the community tank

There are plenty to choose from, but remember that a selection must be based on the size of your tank.

TIGER BARB (*BARBUS TETRAZONA*)

Native to Indonesia, the tiger barb's name suits it well: not only are they striped, but they can also come in different colours, including albino, and red and green. They can be quite the bully and are known to nip the fins of tank mates. Their mature size is about 7cm (2.75 in). They need to be housed in a school of at least six – preferably eight – and although they will spend their time establishing and maintaining their own pecking order and be too busy to nip other fish, it's not a good idea to house them in a tank with slow-moving fish or those with long, trailing fins like guppies, gouramis and angelfish; it's too tempting for them.

CHERRY BARB (*BARBUS TITTEYA*)

Taking their name from the deep red colour of the males at spawning time, the cherry barb from Sri Lanka grows to about 5 cm (2 in). The female is a pale brown with a dark brown stripe running from the snout, through the eye and along the body to the base of the caudal fin. While they will live in a pair in a tank, they are happiest in a small school with plenty of plant cover for shelter: watch them gather in a school and then later go their separate ways to rest on their own. When breeding, the pair swim over fine-leafed plants and deposit one to three eggs at a time on each pass, until up to 300 eggs are laid. The tiny fry hatch out 24 hours later. Beware: the eggs make a tasty treat for the parents!

TOP: TIGER BARB.
BOTTOM: CHERRY BARB.

ROSY BARB (*BARBUS CONCHONIUS*)

The rosy barb, which hails from northern India, Assam and Bengal, is a very hardy little fish – mature size about 7 cm (2.75 in). Ideal for the novice aquarist, they will eat anything from algae and plants to flake, tablet and live food. They're peaceful, tolerant of other species (although they can be boisterous) and mix well with other similar sized barbs. They are constantly on the move, so you need to make sure there is plenty of space for them to swim in and that there are plenty of plants for them to shelter in. Rosy barbs can be kept as a pair but are best in a group of six: make sure to get both male and female, so the boys can display their true colours to the girls when they are fully mature. Rosy barbs breed and lay their eggs in the same manner as cherry barbs, but they take a little longer to hatch. If you do want to breed them, you must remove the eggs from the tank so the parents don't feast on them.

ARULIUS BARB (*BARBUS ARULIUS*)

This gorgeous barb from southern and southeastern India is one of the largest of the barbs, with a mature size of around 12 cm (4.75 in). To keep them successfully, make sure you have a large aquarium because they like to live alongside other medium to large sized species. When mature, the arulius barb develops a blue-purple pattern along the back and an iridescent blue-green spot on the gill cover.

TOP: ROSY BARB.
BOTTOM: LONG-FIN ROSY BARB.

FLYING FOX
(*EPALZEORHYNCHUS KALLOPTERUS*)

This barb originates from Borneo and Sumatra. It has a brown to olive-green back and a yellow longitudinal band with a band of black just beneath. The iris of its eye is bright red and the dorsal, anal and ventral fins have a black bar and a white border. They are great fish to watch: at rest, they like to balance on a rock on their pectoral fins but they also enjoy playing in the oxygenated outflow of the water filter. The flying fox is a very hardy fish that likes dense vegetation, scattered rock and roots to explore: it will rasp algae from the surfaces as well as from the aquarium glass, so it's a useful housekeeper in the tank. It's also very happy in a community tank with other species, but care must be taken because flying foxes are very territorial and will fight members of its own species for territory near the bottom of the tank. So only keep one in a tank of 60 cm (24 in).

ZEBRA DANIO (*DANIO RERIO*)

This slender fish hails from eastern India and Bangladesh and was first introduced to the aquarium in 1905. It's one of the hardiest of fish and is really suitable for the beginner because it is now one of the most extensively farmed tropical freshwater fishes – and one of the least expensive. They grow to about 5 cm (2 in) long. The bodies of the males have a golden background colour marked by four dark blue longitudinal stripes. Its 'cousin', the leopard danio has a similar colour but spots instead of stripes.

TOP: ZEBRA DANIO.

GIANT DANIO (*DANIO AEQUIPINNATUS*)

From Sri Lanka and the west coast of India, the giant danio grows to 10 cm (4 in) and consequently needs accommodating in a large, well-planted tank. This handsome fish needs to be in a school and enjoys swimming in the upper levels of the water near the surface, but it is a very active fish and the school may disturb quieter species in a community tank. Its natural habitat is fast-flowing water, so the aquarium needs to be well aerated for it to thrive. It's a fast swimmer – and a good jumper, so make sure the condensation trays are shut and the lid is on the tank!

HARLEQUIN RASBORA (*TRIGONOSTIGMA HETEROMORPHA*)

One of the most commonly kept rasboras, the harlequin was introduced to aquariums in 1906. Native to Thailand, Malaysia and Indonesia, this rasbora will grow to about 4.5 cm (1.75 in) and has a very distinctive wedge-shaped blue-black marking on the rear part of its silvery body, with a red dorsal fin that becomes golden yellow towards the tips. They should be kept in a small school in a tank with areas of dense vegetation arranged to allow them sufficient space for swimming, most of which takes place in the upper zone of the tank.

TOP: GIANT DANIO.
BOTTOM: HARLEQUIN RASBORA.

your freshwater aquarium

WHITE CLOUD MOUNTAIN MINNOW (*TANICHTHYS ALBONUBES*)

This poetically named minnow is native to China, near Canton, and it is said that a young boy called Tan (hence *Tanichthys* or 'Tan's fish') discovered the fish in 1930 on the White Cloud Mountain in Canton (*albonubes* means 'white cloud'). This is one of the most undemanding of fish to keep in the community tank: it's very tolerant of other fish and of changes in water temperature, but because it comes from mountain streams, it does like to have a portion of the water in the tank changed regularly. It's a beautiful fish with white stripes on its flanks and striking red and white fins. Like danios and rasboras, this minnow likes to be in a school: lonesome individuals pine for company and lose their colour. Expect this minnow to grow to about 4 cm (1.5 in) long.

THE COBITIDAE FAMILY: LOACHES

Loaches are bottom-dwelling carp-like fish related to the Cyprinidae family and are often quiet, peaceful fish well suited to the community tank. They forage on the bottom of the tank among the substrate hoovering up particles of food missed by the other fish. They're also equipped with a strong, trunk-like mouth that pulls snails out of their shells for eating. Some loaches can grow quite large, so while you can keep a few immature and small loaches in a tank, only keep a single mature one. The most popular loaches for the community tank include the very colourful clown loach (*Botia macaranthus*) from Sumatra and Borneo. With its bright orange body and flanks crossed by three broad wedge-shaped black bands the clown loach is an attractive addition to the community tank, but it must be provided with soft sandy areas in the substrate to allow the fish to burrow for live food. They are long-lived fish and although they grow slowly, reaching about 30 cm (12 in) when mature, one clown loach is enough in a tank (of a minimum 60 cm/24 in) or they will fight for territory.

The dwarf (or chain) loach (*Yasuhikotakia sidthimunki*) is a peaceful active fish that is about during the day. It needs to be kept in a group of six so the fish can interact with each other. They will grow to about 3.5 cm (1.25 in). They have a small spine below their eye called a bifid spine that they can erect and lower at will as a form of defence. When they use this spine they sometimes also produce an audible clicking sound. Again they need a soft substrate in which to forage for food but they also do like to rest themselves on broad-leafed plants (such as the Amazon sword plant). These fish don't like going into a newly set up tank system, so ideally you should wait about six months before introducing them.

LIKE BARBS, DANIOS, RASBOAS AND MINNOWS ARE ALSO VERY HARDY FISH AND IDEAL FOR THE COMMUNITY TANK AND FOR THE NOVICE KEEPER. LIKE BARBS, ALL THESE FISH ARE SHOALING FISH SO ARE IDEALLY KEPT WITH 3 OR 4 OTHER FISH OF THE SAME SPECIES.

THE CHARACIDAE FAMILY

This large family of fish has about 200 species in Africa and some 1,000 species in South and Central America and the southern regions of North America. Many are small – or very small fish – with a short dorsal fin, usually an adipose fin and a deeply cleft caudal fin. It's from this family that some of the most popular and vividly coloured schooling fish come: the tetras. Like barbs and rasboras, the tetras are small, peaceful schooling fish that are perfect for the community tank, where their gorgeous jewel-like colours light up the environment. Again, because the tetras are widely farmed, they are inexpensive fish and are well adapted to aquarium life as long as there are plenty of plants to mimic their natural habitat. No community tank is complete without at least one school of beautiful tetras.

CARDINAL TETRA
(PARACHEIRODON AXELRODI)

One of the most popular of all the tetras – and of tropical freshwater aquarium fish – the cardinal tetra, with its iridescent red belly and blue stripe, is luminescent under artificial light. It hails from western Colombia and northeastern Brazil and will grow up to 4 cm or so (1.5 in). They can be a little fussy: don't introduce this fish to a new aquarium system but wait until it has settled down, the water is stablised and there are well-established thickets of planting for the fish to hide in. Single fish will be shy and will hide away – as will duos and trios – but they gain strength and confidence in numbers, so it's worth investing in a school of six or eight. This can be expensive as most of these fish will be wild caught: they are extremely fussy about water conditions for breeding, and in the

TOP: CARDINAL TETRA.

aquarium prefer soft water that is slightly acidic. Tetras are gorgeous – and they give you a very good reason for keeping your logbook of water details up to date.

NEON TETRA (*PARACHEIRODON INNESI*)

Active, colourful and hardy, the neon tetra was originally described only in 1936. Like all tetras, the neon appears to be lit up from within, showing off the blue stripe and red band that extend to the root of its tail. These tetras love swimming in the lower and middle zones of the aquarium but like a tank with a dark substrate and subdued lighting. They will grow up to about 4 cm (1.5 in) long and are happiest in a school of around ten.

BLEEDING HEART TETRA (*HYPHESSOBRYCON ERYTHROSTIGMA*)

With its deep, almost lozenge-shaped body, the bleeding heart tetra is distinguished by the large red mark just behind the gill and below the lateral line that gives the fish its name. This attractive tetra will grow to about 6 cm (2.25 in) and it can be kept in a pair, but if your aquarium is large enough, keep them in a small school. Like many tetras it can be fussy about its water: it prefers water with a pH of 6.5–7.2, but check with your local supplier who may have stock that has become happily accustomed and acclimatised to local water conditions.

TOP: NEON TETRA.
BOTTOM: BLEEDING HEART TETRA.

your freshwater aquarium

GLOWLIGHT TETRA (*HEMIGRAMMUS ERYTHROZONUS*)

A popular aquarium fish since the 1940s, this is one of the most beautiful tetras. It lives mostly in the lower zones of the tank and likes patches of dense vegetation (which also show up their brilliant colour) with plenty of open water for swimming. The ruby-red stripe along the flanks of the glowlight extends through the eye down to the base of the caudal fin, where it terminates in the bright red glowing spot that gives the fish its name. It will grow up to about 4 cm (1.5 in) and enjoys the company of other glowlights, so keep them in a school of at least six.

BLACK NEON TETRA (*HYPHESSOBRYCON HERBERTAXELRODI*)

For a brilliant contrast in the aquarium, the black neon tetra is a superb choice. Originating in the Taquari River in the Matto Grosso region of central Brazil, the black neon is now farmed for the aquarium and, consequently, relatively inexpensive. Although they are very tolerant, don't add them to the tank as your starter fish: you need to wait at six weeks before introducing them, alongside other peaceful species. The wait will be well worth it: black neons have a broad black longitudinal band that extends from behind the gill cover to the base of the tail. Parallel to and above this is a vivid iridescent green-yellow stripe, while its iris is bright blood red above and iridescent green below. They will grow to about 3.5 cm (1.25 in) and are happy to be kept in a small school of four or six other black neons.

NEON TERTRAS ARE A BEAUTIFUL ADDITION TO ANY AQUARIUM.

THE POECILIDAE FAMILY (LIVE-BEARING TOOTHCARPS)

This family of fish, of which there are about 130 known species, are mostly small fish native to the southern United States, Central America (including the West Indies) and south to northern Argentina. Because of their size and gorgeous colours, the live-bearing toothcarps are among the most popular tropical freshwater aquarium fish. Firm favourites are the sailfin molly, the swordtail, the guppy and the platy. Like sharks, rays and skates, live-bearers perform internal fertilisation: the males have a special organ called a gonopodium that is used to deliver packets of sperm to the female. Live-bearing fish produce eggs but the young are completely developed within them. When the egg leaves the body of the mother (usually bigger than males but less highly coloured), the fry discards its 'shell' and is 'born'.

SAILFIN MOLLY
(*POECILIA VELIFERA*)

When mature, this fish will grow to about 18 cm (7 in). Its natural colour is a mix of green, yellow and silver, but a range of colour variations, including gold, marbled and black, have now been bred. It's the male sailfin that has the spectacular long dorsal fin that extends the mottled pattern of the body and is edged with gold. While they will live happily as a pair, the tank does need to be large enough to accommodate them, and they need a good flow of water to keep

TOP: GREEN SAILFIN MOLLY.

them happy. Because of the lovely sailfin, they should not be kept in conditions where fin nippers may bother them. Their upturned mouth is a clear indicator that they feed from the surface of the water.

SWORDTAIL (*XIPHOPHORUS HELLERI*)

The swordtail is a another aquarium favourite and it, too, has been bred in a range of very striking colour combinations: in the wild in Central America the fish is often a dull green but the blood-red coloured swordtail is truly striking. The male will only develop his swordtail when he is fully mature. Swordtails are active fish that swim in the middle and upper zones of the aquarium and will grow to about 10 cm (4 in), so they need plenty of space. They enjoy feeding on flake, plenty of algae and green food. Generally peaceful fish, the males can be antagonistic towards each other, so a mixed pair, or a male and two females, ensures harmony.

TOP: SWORDTAIL.
BOTTOM: LYRETAIL SWORDTAIL.

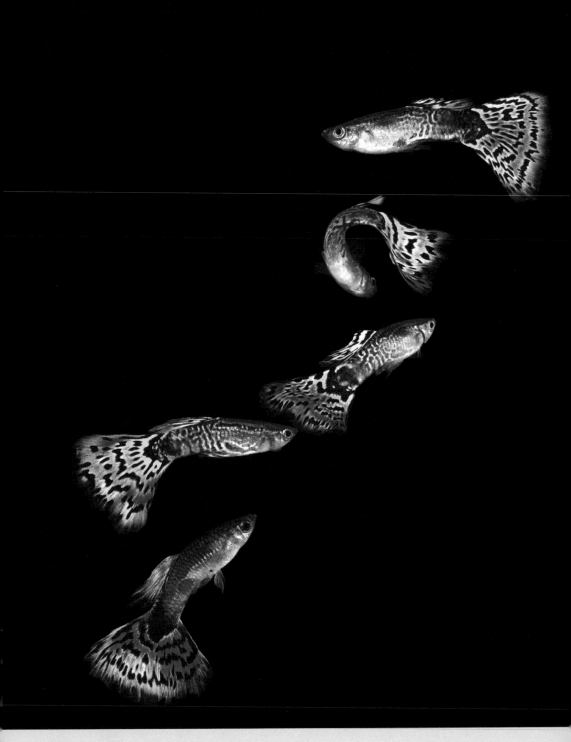

your freshwater aquarium

GUPPY (*POECILIA RETICULATA*)

Sometimes also called the millions fish, the guppy has been selectively bred to provide the aquarium with a vast range of colours and shapes: the males have a fabulous long, flowing caudal fin and often gaudy colours, while the females often are only coloured at their rear and tail. Check out the king cobra guppy and the neon blue! Be sure to buy a pair with both sexes for your tank as the boy needs the girl to show off to! Guppies are originally from Central America but in the aquarium will tolerate quite a wide range of water temperature – between 18–28°C (64–82°F) – and will thrive in hard, neutral to alkaline water. Guppies will grow to about 6 cm (2.25 in) and are very peaceful fish that occupy the middle and upper zones of the aquarium: don't keep them with male Siamese fighting fish or boisterous barbs, however, because if their colouration is too similar, they will mistake each other for rivals and attack.

PLATY (*XIPHOPHORUS MACULATUS*)

The Platy is an excellent 'novice' fish: it adapts very well to aquarium life, is peaceful, and very colourful. Like its 'cousin' the swordtail, the platy has been bred to provide a huge range of variations including the red wagtail, tuxedo, moon, blue hifin and sunset. Keep a pair (a male and a female) and make sure they get plenty of green food or they'll start to nibble at the plants – although they are usually looking for algae and do little damage, you could make sure you plant robust plants such as the Amazon sword plant and Java fern. They will grow to about 6 cm (2.25 in) and long-finned varieties should not be kept with boisterous barbs or male Siamese fighting fish, which may mistake them for rivals.

BEAUTIFUL COLOURS TYPIFY THE POPULAR GUPPY - A
STUNNING ADDITION TO ANY AQUARIUM.

THE ANABANTOID FAMILY (LABYRINTH FISH)

This family of fish, native to Africa and Southeast Asia, all have an accessory respiratory organ – the labyrinth organ – that lies in the gill cavity and allows these fish to take in atmospheric air at the surface of the water and extract the oxygen contained in it. This developed because the water that these fish inhabit in the wild is often poorly oxygenated. In most of the species, the male labyrinth fish builds a floating bubble nest at the water's surface. The nest is a series of bubbles coated with saliva (and often a certain amount of plant matter) and courtship takes place below the nest with the male coiling the female around him and then turning her upside down. The eggs float upwards and land in the bubble nest, where they are guarded by the male. Most of the anabantoids in the aquarium are small, brightly coloured and easy to keep, but they all like mature aquariums, so don't introduce them too early. Among the most popular choices are the Siamese fighting fish and the gouramis.

SIAMESE FIGHTING FISH (*BETTA SPLENDENS*)

Highly ornamental, the male Siamese fighting fish from Southeast Asia is an elongated, laterally compressed fish with a very long anal fin and almost circular caudal fin. They are very beautiful fish and grow to about 7 cm (2.75 in) but unfortunately only live for about two years. A single

TOP: SIAMESE FIGHTING FISH.

male (with one or two females if you wish) will live happily in a community tank, as long as there are no fin nippers. Never keep two males together, or they will become highly aggressive towards each other, and keep a breeding pair in a separate tank on their own. Make sure there are plenty of plants that reach the surface of the water in the tank and also grow some thickets for the fish to hide in. It is vital for these fish to be able to breathe air from the surface, so make sure there is plenty of open space for them.

DWARF GOURAMI (*COLISA LALIA*)

These small gouramis with their humped shoulders are ideal for the peaceful community tank – but don't be tempted to add them to a newly set up system. Wait at least six months before introducing a pair into the tank and pay particular attention to the water quality. Poor water conditions will make the gouramis' fins ragged; they go off their food and start sulking in a quiet part of the tank. In the worst case, they can then develop bacterial infections. The females are more silvery in colour, while the males have red and blue bars along their bodies and will grow to around 5 cm (2 in).

TOP: DWARF GOURAMI.
BOTTOM: NEON BLUE DWARF GOURAMI.

PEARL GOURAMI
(*TRICHOGASTER LEERI*)

At 10 cm (4 in) the pearl gourami is one of the larger aquarium species. It has the most stunning colours and patterns and if they are kept healthy – in a pair in a tank with other peaceful species – they can live for up to eight years. It needs plenty of space in the upper zone of the tank where it can take in atmospheric air and some densely planted areas in which to rest. Pay attention to the water temperature: don't let it fall below 24°C (75°F) or the fish will start to feel the chill, go off their food and sulk; they can also become ill.

BLUE OR THREE SPOT GOURAMI
(*TRICHOGASTER TRICHOPTERUS*)

These are probably the easiest of the gouramis to keep: they are omnivorous and will eat planarian worms, which means you don't have to add chemicals to the water to get rid of them! They get their 'three spot' name because of the two spots on their body, plus their eye. The males are more intensely coloured than the females and when mature develop a more pointed dorsal fin. They are relatively peaceful fish but the males can become aggressive towards each other: a mixed pair will keep the peace.

TOP: PEARL GOURAMI.
BOTTOM: THREE-SPOT GOURAMI.

SILURIFORMES: CATFISH

The Siluriforme order of fish contains around 34 families with about 2,000 species that are distributed worldwide. Most catfish are freshwater fish, although a few are found in marine environment. Their skin is 'naked' or covered with bony plates but never with 'true' scales. They are solitary fish, mostly active at night or at dusk and use their barbels to compensate for their poorly developed eyesight. Of the aquarium catfish, the Corydoras are among the most popular. Because they live at the bottom of the tank, they are sometimes (rather unfairly!) described as hoovers as they forage in the substrate looking

TOP: THE CORYDORAS ARE VERY POPULAR
AQUARIUM FISH - THEY HELP KEEP THE BOTTOM
OF THE TANK CLEAN.

for leftover food. So their delicate barbels are not damaged, the substrate must be soft and sandy.

BRONZE CORYDORAS (*CORYDORAS AENEUS*)

The green-bronze coloured bronze corydoras is an ideal fish for the novice aquarist – and comes with added the benefit of being active during the day! Although they dig into the substrate, which should be soft with rounded particles of sand or fine gravel, these catfish won't dig up the plants. A pair will be happy in a community tank – three would be even nicer (a male and two females) but individuals will also shoal with other Corydoras species.

PANDA CORYDORAS (*CORYDORAS PANDA*)

This attractive catfish is named after its panda-like black mask that runs from the top of its head down through its eyes. These catfish like to be in a small group – lone individuals don't thrive– so a group of three or four is ideal. At maturity, they will be about 5 cm (2 in) long.

TOP: BRONZE CORYDORAS.

STERBA'S CORYDORAS
(*CORYDORAS STERBAI*)

The distinctive and evenly spotted cat-fish is an aquarium favourite. At maturity it will be about 6 cm (2.25 in) and needs a nice open area of substrate around which it can swim with surroundings of roots and caves for shelter.

BRISTLENOSE CATFISH
(*ANCISTRUS TEMMINCKII*)

Distinguished by the magnificent 'whiskers' on its nose, the bristlenose is a suckermouth catfish that is very useful for dealing with algae. However, they are constant grazers, so need to be well provided with green food – or they will eat the plants. Nocturnal in their habits, during the day they need a nice dark cave to rest in and open areas of sandy substrate in which to forage using its fine barbels. These catfish like really clean, clear and well-oxygenated water: if the oxygen levels drop (in hot weather perhaps) they will be found at the surface of the water where the oxygen levels are higher. Make sure that the return oxygenated airflow on the power filter is strong, or provide an additional air pump to keep oxygen levels up.

TOP: STERBA'S CORYDORAS.
BOTTOM: BRISTLENOSE CATFISH.

your freshwater aquarium

THE CICHLIDAE FAMILY

The cichlids comprise about 650 species mostly found in the freshwaters of Africa and Central and South America. When breeding, the males are very territorial, so for this reason, a single pair is enough in the community tank. In some species, the eggs are deposited on rocks, leaves and timber, but other species prefer 'nests' in caves or dig pits in the sandy substrate (which means your plants get uprooted!).

Because of their habits and needs, many species of cichlids are kept in separate species tanks with particular conditions designed to suit the breed, rather than in community tanks, but nonetheless there are some that are well suited and very popular. You may, however, want to wait a while before embarking on life with cichlids – perhaps set up a second, separate species tank and learn more about their fascinating behaviour before introducing them to the community tank.

ANGELFISH (*PTEROPHYLLUM SCALARE*)

Despite their name, angelfish can be devilish: in the community tank they must only be kept with fish they cannot eat! They will feast on small neon and cardinal tetras and so should only be kept with peaceful community fish that are longer than 4 cm (1.5 in). Angels can also be greedy fish: overeating can cause their early demise so keep their diet under strict control. Over the years, angels have been bred to produce many morphs, including gold, black and half-black, along with a range of fin forms – so make sure they are not housed with fin nippers. They need plenty of open water in the middle zone of the tank with broadleafed plants (like the Amazon sword plant) and thickets of greenery at the sides and back. Because of their size – up to about 15 cm (6 in) long and 20cm (8 in) high – angelfish need a big tank –no less than 90 cm (36 in) long and at least 40 cm (16 in) high. These fish like to live in small groups of three to four, and the individuals always maintain a small distance from each other. They don't like lively company, so choose their tank mates with great care.

A FISH ALMOST EVERYONE CAN RECOGNISE, THE ANGELFISH
DOES NOT LIVE UP TO ITS NAME- IT WILL EAT MANY OTHER FISH
IF IT GETS THE CHANCE!

KEYHOLE CICHLID (*CLEITHRACARA MARONII*)

The keyholes are lovely, colourful little fish about 5–6 cm (2.25 in) long. They are very peaceful and adapt well to life in the community tank: their digging is confined to the breeding season and then they are so delicate that they don't uproot plants. If they become nervous or frightened their colouration turns a mottled brown – a useful indicator to the keeper that something is wrong – so provide them with plenty of shelter where they can hide themselves away if they feel threatened. They occupy the lower and middle zones of the tank and are fussy about the water quality – a portion should be changed every three weeks or so to keep them happy and healthy. A pair in the tank will establish their territory to raise a family but young fish will not be sexable so you should start with 3–5 young fish to give the best chance of a pair. Adult males are more colourful and slimmer than the females with their anal and dorsal fins extended into points.

These are just a few of the most popular freshwater tropical fish suitable for aquarium life. As you gain in experience and knowledge – and perhaps in the number of tanks you set up – you can extend your range even

TOP: ABOVE: KEYHOLE CICHLID.

further. Before you do though, you need to be armed with important information about feeding the fish you already have, and the routine maintenance you need to do to take care of the fish's environment.

As you have discovered, the range of tropical freshwater fish is vast and so too are their natural habitats and the diets they enjoy. In the wild the fish would swim about looking for their next meal: in the confined environment of the aquarium, they rely on the keeper to feed them. A lot of time, energy and research have gone into fish nutrition and it's now possible to feed fish a healthy diet using commercially produced fish food. This has been developed to cater for all manner of fish needs and eating habits and is available freeze-dried, in tablets, in dried form and as floating food sticks and sinking granules.

OTHER POPULAR MEMBERS OF THE CICHLID
FAMILY INCLUDE THE DISCUS FISH (TOP) AND
THE BUTTERFLY CICHLID (BOTTOM)

feeding and caring for your fish

your freshwater aquarium

Do not overfeed!

Although fish can become bored of the same food day after day and go off their food for a while, the real danger for their health is overfeeding. Overfeeding doesn't mean overweight or obese fish – apart from one or two species they don't overindulge like humans – the danger comes from the food that is not eaten. Leftovers will decay in the aquarium and sooner or later will pollute the water. The cardinal rule is: feed little and often. The fish should eat up all their food in a matter of minutes, so if you share responsibility for feeding make sure everyone knows when feeding time is, what quantities and type of food are required and that no one adds any more to the tank. It's important that you feed the fish when you have time to watch them and make sure they are all eating: refusal to eat is a sure indication of either illness or poor water conditions.

FEEDING TIMES

A feed in the morning, at noon and at night – provided only small amounts of food are given at each time – is a useful pattern for both the fish and the keeper. The fish will get used to regular times, so make it part of a scheduled routine. The feed just before 'lights out' is particularly important so that fish with nocturnal habits don't go hungry through their period of activity. A well-looked-after aquarium can be left to itself for 2–3 days without food, but ideally someone should be monitoring the tank for water quality, to make sure all the equipment is working properly and that there are no dead fish in the tank. If you do go away, make up parcels of food in labelled (day, date and time of feed) envelopes using a little less food than normal so your stand-in knows exactly what and when to give the fish. An alternative is an automatic fish feeder but this does not remove the need for someone to keep an eye on the tank conditions.

DRIED FISH FOOD IS THE STAPLE DIET OF THE AQUARIUM INHABITANTS
AND COMES IN A RANGE OF FORMS FROM FLOATING FLAKES AND SINKING
PELLETS THAT ARE DESIGNED SO DIFFERENT FISH WITH DIFFERENT FEEDING
HABITS CAN FEED EASILY.

When not to feed!

• Don't feed your fish if you don't have the time to watch them feeding to see whether all of the fish in the tank are eating healthily.
• Never feed your fish if you have just switched on the lights: wait at least 30 minutes so the fish are fully awake and alert – and hungry for their food.
• Never feed the fish if you have just undertaken some aquarium maintenance – cleaning, changing water, changing/replacing the filter medium. These procedures unsettle the fish and they will need time to settle down again. They won't eat if they're upset so all the food will be wasted and will need removing from the tank, thereby causing them more upset.
• Never switch off the filter when you feed the fish!

How often to feed

The frequency with which fish are fed depends on their size: small fish require several small feeds each day, whereas large fish need more substantial feeds but less often. In a community tank of small fish, start off small and gradually increase the portions as the tank matures: start with one feed every other day for the first week and then increase this to two or three small feeds a day after two months or so.

How much to feed

The simple rule here is that it's better to give less food to the fish rather than too much. In the wild, fish will go for days without food: in the tank they get used to the routine and they do learn when feeding time is. When a school of fish rush to the front pane of the tank when they see you, it's because they'd like to think you were going to feed them, not because they need feeding! Animals that gorge on food are highly susceptible to disease so, the rules for feeding are:
• Only offer as much food as the fish will eat in a short time: flakes of food should sink no deeper than one-third of the height of the tank and tablets should be provided for bottom feeders. This way there is no waste to affect the water quality.
• Feed small portions, one at a time.
• Feed flakes as the basic diet and offer tasty variety foods in frozen or freeze-dried form only as a weekly or fortnightly treat.
• Don't crumble the flakes: the fish need to work for their food.
• Never create a stock of food in the tank: this will simply rot and poison the water.

THE RANGE OF FOOD FOR FISH IS EXTRAORDINARY: FLAKES, PELLETS, AND ALGAE WAFERS ALL NUTRITIONALLY BALANCED FOR OPTIMUM HEALTH. ALWAYS READ THE LABELS, AND JUST LIKE 'HUMAN FOOD', MAKE SURE THE FOOD IS KEPT FRESH AND USED BEFORE THE SELL BY DATE.

your freshwater aquarium

What to feed

Don't be tempted to use 'wild food' – food you have caught for the fish yourself from rivers and ponds. First of all you may be in breach of conservation laws and secondly – and more dangerously to your fish – you may inadvertently introduce dangerous pathogens into your tank. Using quality foods offered in stores for fish is both safe and provides a varied diet.

DRY FOOD

Dried fish food is the 'nuts and bolts' of a fish's diet and is available in a variety of forms from tablets to flakes and granulated pellets. It contains all the vital nutrients in sufficient quantities, as well as roughage to keep those piscine intestines in peak condition! Flaked food is available in various sizes suited to the size of the fish – and their mouths. Don't forget always to bear in mind each species' special requirements: those that like a vegetarian diet will need flakes with a large proportion of green stuff, so make sure you read the labels or ask for advice. Dried food in tablet form is often used for fish that are bottom feeders: you can let them drop to the bottom of the tank. Sinking granules are most suitable for bottom-dwelling catfish who will snuffle about, using their barbels to find them in the soft, sandy substrate.

There are also tablets that can be stuck to the glass pane of the aquarium where they can be nibbled at by the mid-zone community fish! Granulated pellets are also known as crumb food: although it's of very high nutritive value, many fish simply turn their noses up at it to begin with, but in time, they do become accustomed to it. For variety, it's a good idea to feed the fish flakes and pellets alternatively.

Floating food sticks look like miniature versions of humans' healthy bran cereal: these are particularly suited to the larger barbs that feed from the surface of the water.

FISH FLAKES COME IN A RANGE OF SIZES TO SUIT DIFFERENT SIZED FISH AND IN A RANGE OF 'DIETARY REQUIREMENTS': SOME HAVE MORE GREEN CONTENT TO SUIT HERBIVOROUS FISH.

FREEZE-DRIED AND FROZEN FOOD

Freeze-dried food consists of food animals – such as mosquito larvae and tubifex (tube-dwelling worms that live in the mud of often heavily polluted waters) that have been frozen in a way that results in a dry product. Such animal food in its live form might introduce diseases so it has been gamma-irradiated to kill fish pathogens before being freeze-dried or frozen. Frozen food is often sold in sheets divided into little cubes of about 1 cubic cm. With small fish that run the risk of swallowing a whole cube, put the frozen cube on the water surface where it will thaw slowly, appearing to be tantalisingly alive and moving, and so only attracting fish that respond to movement in their natural prey in the wild. With larger fish, always thaw the cube in a saucer before adding it to the tank.

• As with human food, never refreeze already thawed-out frozen foods.

• Freeze-dried and frozen animal foods are a 'treat' for fish and should be given as a supplement to, and not in place of, their regular flake food diet.

SPECIAL TREATS

Like humans, many fish enjoy the occasional treat of fresh fruit or vegetables: some algae eaters in particular will graze on a slice of cucumber, a piece of lettuce or a frozen pea. It's a good idea to wait several months until the tank is fully mature before you try offering this type of food to your fish. When you do, make sure the vegetables are thoroughly washed to remove any traces of pesticides and dirt. Such greens are especially useful to the 'adolescent' herbivorous fish – and it stops them from devouring your aquatic plants. You can buy lettuce grips to hold such items of food (lettuce leaves will float and are often ignored by the fish!) and they should be placed in a visible part of the tank where you can monitor them for freshness and remove them if the food is not eaten. Offer a frozen pea by popping it from its outer skin between your finger and thumb. Discard the skin – fish don't like them and small fish can get them attached to their fins – and drop the pea in the tank. Only ever feed fresh greens and remember that these are supplementary treats to their regular diet of prepared dried foods. Any uneaten greens – including peas at the bottom on the substrate – should be removed.

Vitamin concentrates in liquid form are available and will help meet the fish's requirements: some of these are added to the tank water, while others can be sprinkled over frozen food before offering it to the tank. Ask your aquarium supplier for details, follow the instructions on the label for delivery methods and don't exceed the recommended dosage. You might think one little drop won't make a difference, but one drop in an aquarium is like a large bucket of cold water added to a hot bathtub – and it will alter the chemical make-up of the water.

FROZEN OR FREEZE DRIED FISH FOOD IS A 'TASTY TREAT'- AN OCCASIONAL SUPPLEMENT
TO THEIR REGULAR DIET OF DRIED FISH FOOD.

RUTO · FROZEN FISHFOOD

DAPHNIA

High protein food for all kinds of fish

Only the best for yo...

GROSS...

GROSS WEIGHT ± 100 G.

LIVE FOOD

Daphnia (water fleas) and bloodworms can be bought live from aquarium suppliers but they are also available frozen or freeze-dried (see above), which is often more convenient – and in many instances, much safer, as the fresh versions won't have been gamma-irradiated. Daphnia is well suited to small fish, while larger fish relish the bloodworms; both are sold in plastic bags filled with water. You need to strain the contents of the bag through a very fine meshed net so you are only giving the live food to the fish and nothing else: Do not put the water in the aquarium! You can often buy bloodworms dry packed in layers of damp paper. Again these should be considered a treat and offered only once a week or every ten days.

Top tips
• Just as you wouldn't want to eat leftover fish food, don't ever give your fish your kitchen leftovers! These can rapidly alter and impair the water quality and be lethal to the fish.
• Keep the fish on strict diets: when you buy new fish, ask the retailer what they have been feeding on and continue with the same food at home. Any changes you make to their diet should be made slowly and gradually.

FISH HOUSED IN AQUARIA DO BECOME ACCUSTOMED TO THE ROUTINE OF FEED-
ING TIME AND WILL RACE TO THEIR FAVORITE FEEDING SPOT IN THE TANK. THE
FREQUENCY WITH WHICH THEY ARE FED DEPENDS ON THEIR SIZE: SMALL FISH
NEED SEVERAL SMALL FEEDS EACH DAY WHILE LARGER FISH NEED BIGGER FEEDS
BUT LESS OFTEN. ANY UNEATEN FOOD SHOULD BE REMOVED IMMEDIATELY OR IT
WILL ROT AND FOUL THE WATER.

Healthcare –
and health scares

Under normal conditions, a fish's natural immune system helps them to fight off infections and disease. But, in spite of all the best efforts, the aquarium is not a natural environment but an artificial habitat that attempts to imitate the real. At some stage or another fish in the aquarium will become sick and you must be prepared: nearly all the common ailments are treatable and the most common problems are often caused by a lack of careful, routine aquarium cleaning and maintenance. The main problems occur when fish are stressed or injured or the background levels of harmful pollutants and bacteria rise to dangerous levels. Making sure that the aquarium is not overstocked with fish or plants, taking care when introducing new fish into the tank (quarantining them first is a good idea), constant vigilance over water conditions and good aquarium maintenance will all help to significantly lessen the occurrence and severity of any sicknesses.

SUDDEN DEATHS

Diseases usually take some time to develop and affect the fish: look out for signs such as loss of appetite and any obvious physical symptoms. Sudden deaths are usually the result of pollutants in the water that may not be easy to test for, but you can buy special polishing media for filters to remove any unusual pollutants

THERE ARE NUMEROUS PRODUCTS AVAILABLE TO HELP KEEP THE WATER'S MINERAL AND pH LEVELS AT A CONSTANT AND SAFE LEVEL FOR THE FISH. THERE ARE VITAMIN TONICS THAT ARE ADDED TO THE TANK WATER TO HELP MAINTAIN FISH VITALITY, AND IN CASE OF ILLNESS, SOLUBLE MEDICATIONS. IN ALL INSTANCES, SEEK PROFESSIONAL ADVICE FIRST AND ALWAYS READ THE INSTRUCTIONS AS TO DOSAGES.

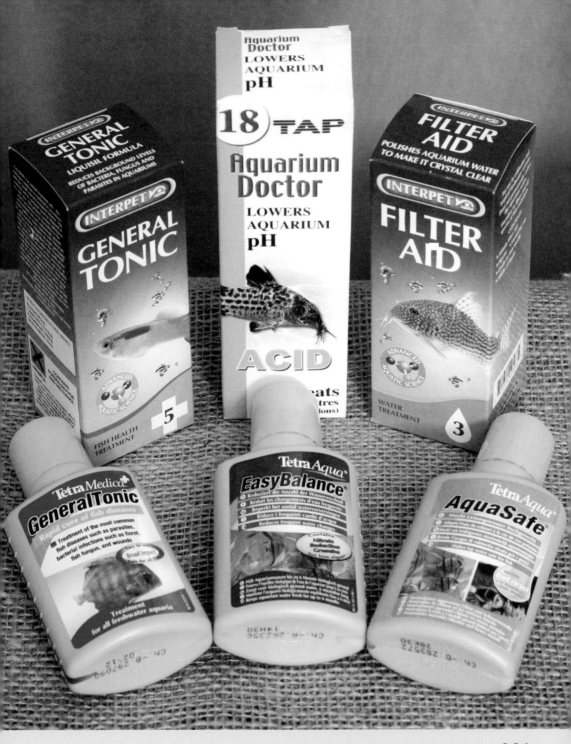

A SEPARATE TANK

A small separate treatment tank should be set up and run in, ready to receive any patients. This tank doesn't need to be fully furnished, but it should be comfortable enough to provide the fish with their preferred habitat – a rock or two for shelter, a substrate of fine gravel or sand, a 'cave' (a small, new and scrubbed clean terracotta flower pot on its side is good), and one or two potted (but not planted) plants will make them feel secure. Place the thermostat away from the tank base so the fish don't hide underneath it, where they may get burned, and remove the activated charcoal from the filter: leaving this in will absorb any medication added to the tank and reduce its effectiveness. And don't forget to add a condensation hood. The treatment tank can be used as an emergency nursery should any of your fish produce a brood in the community tank, and it's also a good idea to use it to quarantine any new fish you have purchased so they don't introduce any sickness into the existing community.

Locate the treatment tank in a quiet spot or on a shelf beneath your main tank. Affix a sheet of brown paper to the front of the tank so the fish are not disturbed by activity in the room and the light is a little more subdued. Peel back part of the paper two or three times a day to check on the patients' progress.

HYGIENE IN THE HOME

Infection can be spread from one tank to another so make sure all your equipment is scrupulous cleaned and avoid using a single net to catch fish between the different tanks. When a fish is moved from a main tank to the treatment tank, the net must be washed thoroughly afterwards and disinfected. Do not under any circumstances transfer water from the treatment tank to the main tank.

CONTAMINANTS

Just as our air and environment can be polluted, so too can the aquarium: cigarette smoke, aerosol sprays – including household cleaners, deodorants and perfumes – the fumes from cooking, paint, furniture polish and atmospheric pollution, such as that from car exhaust fumes, are all sucked into the tank water by the air pump. It's also possible for small particulates like soot and cement to get into the tank. The condensation tray and the hood will help to reduce the amounts of contaminants, which is why they are important pieces of aquarium equipment and should be shut immediately after any ingress into the tank has been made.

'YOU ARE WHAT YOU EAT'

A diet full of the vital nutrients, vitamins and minerals is necessary for good fish health: just as in human beings, vitamin or mineral deficiencies can be the cause of illness and supplements may be needed to bring the fish back to full health. If your fish are exhibiting signs of illness or distress, then look at their diet.

PLANTS AND FISH DISEASE

Often plants do not develop such visible signs of disease as the fish but they should have been carefully prepared before being placed in the tank and monitored during the running in period before the first fish were introduced. Snail's eggs are the most common stowaways on plants, and if left, there will be an infestation of snails very soon. Make sure any plants you buy are free from eggs – pick them off and rinse the plants thoroughly under running water.

STRESS MEANS DISTRESS

Stress is the major cause of sickness in the aquarium and can be the result of a number of factors:
• Transporting the fish from the store to their new home.
• Sudden changes in water conditions.
• Inappropriate décor: not enough hiding or resting places.
• Bullying by larger or more aggressive fish.
• Fluctuations in water temperature.
• Too many fish for the size of tank.
• Poor water quality.

Before you treat any symptoms of illness it is vital to find and rectify the cause: as long as stress or poor water conditions persist, treatments are ineffective.

IN SOME INSTANCES A FISH MAY NEED TO BE REMOVED FROM THE COMMUNITY TANK AND ISOLATED: THIS MAY BE WHILE IT IS TREATED MEDICALLY AND APART FROM THE REST OF THE COMMUNITY, OR AFTER SPAWNING, WHERE ONE OR MORE PARENTS IS REMOVED IN ORDER THAT THEY DO NOT EAT THEIR OFFSPRING. A SECOND FURNISHED TANK KEPT IN READINESS TO RECEIVE ITS TEMPORARY GUEST IS ADVISED.

TREATING IN THE TANK

Before you carry out any treatment of sick fish, carry out a basic maintenance of the tank and then remove any carbon media from the filter since this will absorb any medication. Some treatments will lower the oxygen level in the water so it's important to keep the water moving and, if possible, increase the level of aeration. Read the manufacturer's instructions carefully and follow them fully, and always carry out the entire course of treatment: some diseases have a life cycle; the treatments are designed to treat and prevent reinfection.

Dilute the correct amount of medication according to the manufacturer's instructions: dilution before adding to the tank means that the medication is dispersed evenly and localised hot spots of high concentration are avoided.

When a course of treatment is fully complete, carry out a small water change and replace the carbon in the filter – use new activated carbon to avoid re-contaminating the water. Avoid using two treatments at the same time – but you can continue to use dechlorinators or plant fertilisers.

USE YOUR LOGBOOK

Keeping a record of conditions and problems in the tank in your logbook is sensible: it stops you panicking and by writing down information you are more likely to think clearly and find the root cause of any problem more quickly.

Prepare a questionnaire, ready for answers in the event of a problem:

How experienced am I? If you are new to keeping tropical freshwater fish then a problem may feel like staring disaster in the face: ask for help and advice from your aquarium supplier, enthusiasts or club members who will help you.

When did the problem start? Keeping a log means you will have an accurate start date for problems that may correspond with, for example, new additions of fish to the tank, a missing maintenance, a possible overfeed, or a possible, overlooked fault in a piece of equipment (heaterstat, power filter).

TREATMENT AGAINST SNAILS WHOSE EGGS HAVE OFTEN BEEN INTRODUCED TO THE TANK ON THE LEAVES OF PLANTS AND FOR FUNGAL INFECTIONS ON FISH ARE READILY AVAILABLE. EACH TIME SUCH A TREATMENT IS ADMINISTERED TO THE TANK, A RECORD OF IT SHOULD BE MADE IN A LOG BOOK SO PROGRESS CAN BE CHECKED.

Local tap water conditions? Check the condition of the water that comes out of your tap. Your local water company may have flushed the main drains to clean and kill bacteria: if you carried out a water change then the tap water you used may not have been conditioned properly. Test the tap water for:
- pH values
- hardness – total (GH)
- carbonate (KH)
- nitrate (NO_3)

Water conditions in the tank? Check and note each of the following:
- pH value
- hardness – total (GH)
- carbonate (KH)
- ammonia (NH_3)
- nitrite (NO_2)
- nitrate (NO_3)
- copper
- temperature
- stocking levels: species and sizes
- tank volume and surface area
- method of filtration
- time since setting up and running in system was completed

Date and extent of routine maintenance? When did you last…
- make a partial water change?
- undertake filter maintenance?

How long is the aeration and filter left running each day? Fish panting for air at the water's surface may be gasping for oxygen because of an excess of carbon dioxide in the water.

When did you last…
- introduce new fish?
- introduce new plants?
- introduce new tank decorations?
- use live food ? Which type was it?

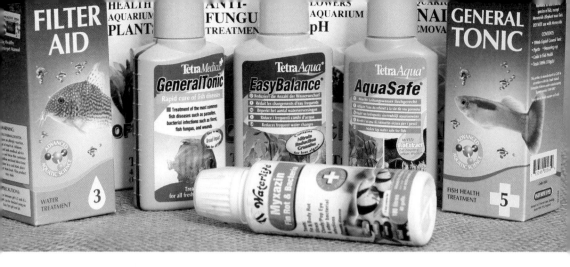

Type and brand(s) of foods used, and frequency of feeding?

Has any new equipment been used in the tank?

Have you painted the room that the tank is located in? Could aerosols, air freshener sprays or cigarette smoke have contaminated the tank?

Any recent use of disease treatments or water treatments? If so, when? And were the doses correct?

Has anything been done to the tank which is out of the ordinary? Ask neighbours if they have been doing any building work or DIY while you were out – the fish may have been stressed by vibrations caused by mechanical equipment.

What are the symptoms of the affected fish? See below for common ailments and symptoms.

Which are the worst-affected species?

What species are NOT affected at this time?

ABOVE: KEEPING THE TANK, THE WATER AND ITS INHABITANTS HEALTHY AND HAPPY IS GREATLY AIDED IF ROUTINE AND REGULAR HOUSEKEEPING CHORES ARE DONE AND ATTENTION PAID TO HYGIENE TO AVOID ANY CROSS CONTAMINATION.

Common ailments, their symptoms and treatments

This is a brief outline of some of the most common ailments and disorders: for any suspected problems that are beyond the scope of this section always refer to a more knowledgeable source: a more experienced fellow enthusiast, a club, your local aquatic supplier or a vet.

Note

To spot-treat an affected fish, carefully paint the affected area of the fish using a small, very soft artist's paintbrush dipped into the medication. Follow the instructions on the medicine label carefully. You may need to repeat this treatment regularly until the condition is cured.

To treat the whole tank, dilute the correct amount of medication according to the manufacturer's instructions and pour gently into the tank. Pour evenly and slowly across the entire length: dilution before adding to the tank means that the medication is dispersed evenly and localised hot spots of high concentration are avoided.

WHITE SPOT DISEASE (*ICHTHYOPHTHIRIASIS*)

This is the most common parasitic disease and can affect every fish in the tank: fortunately it's easy to diagnose and easy to treat. It's caused by a parasite that spends most of its time under the skin of the fish until it matures and becomes visible (as white spots). The parasite then breaks out and falls to the bottom of the tank, where it forms cysts. In each cyst, cell division takes place and produces 1,000 new parasites. When the cyst bursts, the new parasites infect host fish. It's during this free-swimming stage that the treatment is most effective, eradicating the parasites.

Look for: Small, sugar-grain-sized white spots on the bodies and fins of fish.
What to do: Treat the whole tank using a proprietary white spot cure, following the instructions carefully.

FUNGUS (*SAPROLEGNIA*)

Fungus attacks fish that are already weakened by physical attacks (from males of the same species or by larger, more aggressive fish and by fin nipping), parasitic attacks or poor conditions. Fungus is a secondary infection that gets in the wounds when the mucus covering of the fish has been damaged.

Look for: Fluffy, cotton-wool-like growths on the body and/or fins.
What to do: For minor outbreaks, remove the affected fish to a treatment tank and spot-treat the affected area with a proprietary aquarium fungicide. For a major outbreak, treat the whole aquarium. Above all, remedy the cause of the injuries that are allowing fungus to form.

MOUTH FUNGUS, OR MOUTH ROT

Similar in appearance to fungus (see above), it can be a fungal infection, but is often caused by a different slime bacteria (*Flexibacter culumnaris*), so a treatment for body fungus won't be effective on this bacterial infection. However, you can get a treatment that will tackle both.

Look for: Cotton-wool-like growths around the mouth.
What to do: Use a treatment that tackles both fungal and bacterial infections.

VELVET DISEASE

Velvet disease is caused by a skin parasite called Oodinium, which undergoes an encystment stage. Treatment is similar to that for white spot disease.

Look for: Fine gold spots giving a fish a 'dusty' appearance.
What to do: Treat with a targeted anti-parasitic remedy.

FIN ROT/TAIL ROT

This is a problem caused largely by poorly maintained tanks. If caught early, a simple water change and overhaul of the filter system will often rectify the problem. It can also be caused by fin nibblers and bullying by bigger species, allowing bacteria to gain a hold on the injured fins. Become familiar with the shape of your fish's fins: they are normally smooth around the edges, although some may be naturally scalloped.

Look for: Degeneration of the tissue between the individual rays of the fins, so the rays stick out at the edges of the fins.
What to do: In a simple case change the water and overhaul the filter system. If a fish is being bullied, you must rehouse the offender. In more advanced cases, spot-treatment individual fish or, depending how many fish are affected, treat the whole tank with an aquarium bactericide.

RAGGED FINS/TORN OR SPLIT FINS

Ragged, split or torn edges to the fins may be caused by other fish, particularly fin nibblers. Watch to see which fish is the bully and remove it. If the victim is fit and well, the fins should repair themselves, but keep an eye open for any bacterial or fungus infection, e.g., redness or soreness, and treat accordingly.

DROPSY

Sometimes a fish's body becomes bloated to such a degree that its scales start to protrude outwards. This is caused by an internal parasite that causes the body cavities to fill with liquid. This fluid can infect other fish.

Look for: Swelling scales protruding like pinecones.
What to do: Isolate the affected fish in a treatment tank and administer a proprietary internal bacterial treatment.

SKIN AND GILL FLUKES

Skin flukes are parasites called Gyrodactylus that frequently rest near or on the surface of the fish's skin. Gill flukes are flatworms called Dactylogyrus that hook themselves onto the fish's gills. Gill flukes produce eggs that hatch into larvae that in turn find new host fish to infect.

Look for: Fading colours and general feebleness.
What to do: Treat the whole aquarium – check that the plant life will not be harmed by the dosages needed.

SLIMY SKIN

Patches of slime on a fish's body are the result of the immune system responding to the skin parasites Chilodonella and *Ichthyobod costia*.

Look for: Thin grey-coloured patches of slime on the body and folded fins: affected fish also often display erratic, flicking swimming behaviour.
What to do: Treat the whole tank with a proprietary anti-parasitic remedy.

EYE INFECTIONS

Cloudy or protruding eyes (pop eyes) may be due to several causes, including fungus, bacterial infections, eye flakes and even fish tuberculosis. Most often, though, swollen eyes are seen in fish that have Dropsy (see above), so treatment for this will alleviate the eye trouble.

RAPID GILL MOVEMENTS

This type of activity may be a sign of deteriorating water conditions – especially high ammonia levels and/or nitrite levels. It can also be caused by a bacterial or parasite infection.

Look for: More rapid than normal gill movement; any other signs of bacterial infection on skin or fins.
What to do: Check and repair any deficiencies in the water quality: if the water is OK, then treat with a proprietary antibacterial or external parasite remedy.

Always remember to read the instructions before undertaking any treatment. If you are in doubt about any symptoms, always consult a specialist such as a vet.

> **Tip:** Prevention is always better than cure: many of the common illnesses mentioned above can be avoided, providing routine and careful tank maintenance is undertaken. Good housekeeping and active observation on the part of the keeper will reduce the number of incidents and the severity of any outbreaks of sickness.

DISPATCHES

Occasionally the aquarist will be faced with an unexplained death: this happens to even the most experienced aquarium keeper and it may be that the fish has simply died of old age. At some point you may be faced also with the need to dispatch a fish because of severe illness. The quickest and most humane method is to sever the spinal cord just behind the head by cutting down with a very sharp knife. If you cannot do this yourself, then take your fish to a vet.

Note: Do not dispose of sick or dying fish by flushing them down the lavatory or by any other method that would cause a long, painful and inhumane death.

Routine maintenance

Regular and routine maintenance of the aquarium is relatively easy but vital, to keep the tank and its inhabitants healthy. Creating a timetable outlining the daily, weekly, monthly, half-yearly or annual maintenance procedures is a good way to keep track of what you need to do – and to make sure you don't forget anything.

Warning! Water and electricity don't mix! Before undertaking any maintenance, turn off the electricity supply and unplug the device.

CHANGING THE WATER

Water changes are needed to reduce the nitrates that can build up in a tank. The volume and frequency of water changes depend on these nitrate levels, so regular water testing is essential.

To make a water change you'll need a bucket (the one kept specially for use with your aquarium and not any old household bucket!); a length of siphon tubing (clear plastic is best so you can see the flow and make sure that you haven't sucked up a little fish as well!) and a siphon starter (so you avoid ending up with a mouthful of fish tank water when you start the process by sucking on the tube).
• Set the bucket on the floor.
• Place one end of the tube in the tank.

PART OF THE ROUTINE TANK MAINTENANCE INVOLVES REGULAR CHANGING OF PART OF THE WATER. A PROPORTION OF 'OLD WATER' IS REMOVED AND REPLACED WITH NEW, DE-CHLORINATED WATER THAT IS BROUGHT UP TO ROOM TEMPERATURE BEFORE BEING ADDED TO THE TANK BY GENTLY POURING FROM A JUG.

your freshwater aquarium

- Place the other end – with the siphon starter – in your mouth and suck!
- As soon as water enters the tube from the tank, place the sucking end in the bucket. Make sure you don't suck up any little fish and try not to upset the bucket all over the floor.

Aim to replace 15–20% of the water every two weeks. Take new water from the cold tap, treat it with a dechlorinator and leave it to warm up to room temperature before adding it slowly to the tank by pouring in with a jug.

HOOVERING THE SUBSTRATE

Much of the solid organic waste – including uneaten food – in an aquarium will sink to the bottom and end up in the substrate. Live plants in the aquarium use this waste as a source of food, but in open areas it can build up to dangerous levels, encourage algae growth and lead to a harmful deterioration in water quality. There are special hand-held gravel-cleaning devices that disturb the waste particles and suck them up from the substrate: these are lightweight devices that don't rough up the substrate too much, causing a cloud of dust, but check that no small fish have been sucked up too! Give the substrate a good going over once a month as part of your routine maintenance.

KEEPING THE FILTER CLEAN

The power filter is the aquarium's lungs: it needs to be cleaned regularly so that trapped waste matter doesn't build up and clog the system. Internal filters should be cleaned every two weeks; external filters can be cleaned once a month. Remember to rinse the filter foam and other media in water taken from the aquarium. Don't use tap water: it will destroy the vital beneficial bacterial colony that lives on the foam. Only replace half of the bacterial foam or medium at a time: this will leave enough bacteria in place while the new piece of filter medium is colonised. One month later, replace the other half. (Filter media foam needs replacing when it no longer returns to shape after being squeezed.) If your filter contains activated carbon, a new – thoroughly rinsed – batch should be installed every few months.

A USEFUL TOOL IS A SUBSTRATE VACUUM: MUCH OF THE SOLID WASTE IN AN AQUARIUM WILL SINK TO THE BOTTOM AND LODGE BETWEEN THE GRAVEL PARTICLES WHERE IT ROTS. IF NOT REMOVED, THE NITRATE LEVELS IN THE WATER CAN RISE DANGEROUSLY. SMALL HAND-HELD 'GRAVEL HOOVERS' GENTLY DISTURB THE SUBSTRATE AND SUCK UP WASTE MATERIALS: A ONCE A MONTH CLEAN UP OF THE SUBSTRATE SHOULD KEEP THE 'CARPET' NICE AND CLEAN.

MAINTENANCE TIMETABLE

DAILY
- Remove any uneaten food.
- Check the water temperature: heaterstats don't require maintenance; they either work or they don't, so keep a spare handy.
- Check the equipment is working: filter, air pump, lights.
- Count the number of fish – look for missing or dead fish (or any extras).
- Check the fish over for signs of illness.
- Check the planting for any rot or uprooted pants.
- Remove dead leaves floating on water.

EVERY 7–14 DAYS
- Make a partial water change.
- Remove any dead vegetation.
- Remove debris from substrate.
- Clean condensation tray or cover glass to remove salts and algae.
- Clean inside glass of aquarium to remove excess algae.
- Feed plants with liquid fertiliser.
- Gently wiggle fine-leafed plants to shake out any trapped detritus.

MONTHLY
- Clean the power filter.
- Vacuum-clean the gravel substrate.

EVERY 6 MONTHS
- Fully service the air pump.
- Replace one half of the bacterial filter medium or foam (allow one month before replacing the other half).
- Service the filter motor.
- Replace lighting tubes (at least once a year).

AS REQUIRED
- Replenish any tablet fertilisers (if these have been used).
- Trim tall plants to stop them blocking out the light from lower growing ones (you can use the cuttings to propagate new plants).
- Check the conditions in the treatment or quarantine tank: make sure everything is working properly in case you need to house new arrivals or treat existing fish.

AQUA 30 - SPECIAL OFFER PRICE!!!

Including Filter & Light

Coldwater Setup - WAS £44.99, NOW £39.99

Tropical Setup - WAS £54.99, NOW £20.05

your freshwater aquarium

Conclusion

Once you have gained some experience in keeping healthy tropical freshwater fish, you may want to develop your interest further and set up a second community aquarium with larger fish. Or maybe a specialist tank dedicated to a particular species – cichlids perhaps – which requires quite specialist attention. You might also want to try breeding fish or you might like to develop a tropical saltwater aquarium or an aquarium-terrarium with a separate land section for amphibious animals.

Whatever you choose, remember that you are ultimately responsible for the care, health and well-being of all the plants and animals in your tanks: make sure you do sufficient research into the species of fish that interest you and become familiar with their particular needs – water, temperature, diet, habitat preferences and so on.

Build up a library of useful books, including a good, well-illustrated encyclopaedia of fish, and join a club so you can share knowledge – and worries – with other enthusiasts and experienced aquarists.

If you are a complete novice at fish keeping and this is the first book you have read on tropical freshwater fish, then before you buy any equipment – or indeed any fish – take a look at some of the texts suggested on page 224. You may find some of these very helpful before you commit to keeping tropical freshwater fish.

Please do not buy any fish on a whim! Make sure you are sufficiently genned up about them so you can look after them properly. Ask yourself if you are now both still interested in the subject and prepared to undertake the care and maintenance that keeping these animals requires.

index

Recommended Reading

About Pets: The Tropical Fish (2003) About Pets Books

Axelrod, H. et al. Exotic Tropical Fishes (1981) T.F.H

Dal Vesco et al. Life in the Aquarium (1975) Octopus Publishing

Frank, Dr. S. Illustrated Encyclopaedia of Aquarium Fish (1980) Octopus Publishing

Gilbert, J. The Complete Aquarists Guide to Freshwater Fish (1981) Peter Lowe

Hervey, and Hems A Guide to Freshwater Aquarium Fishes (1973) Hamlyn

Hiscock, P. Gold Medal Guide: Golden Tips for your First Tropical Aquarium (2007) Interpret Press

Mills, D. Veevers, G., and Campbell, D. G. The Interpret Encyclopaedia of Freshwater Tropical Aquarium Fishes (2003) Interpret Press

Ramshort, Dr. J.D. van Complete Aquarium Encyclopaedia of Tropical Freshwater Fishes (1978) Elsevier Phaidon

Sandford, G. A Practical Guide to Setting Up Your Tropical Freshwater Aquarium and An Essential Guide to Choosing Your Tropical Freshwater Fish in the Tankmaster Series published by Interpret Books

Stadelmann, P. and Finley, L. Tropical Fish: A Complete Pet Owner's Manual (2003) Barron's

Thabrew, Dr. V. de Popular Aquarium Plants (1981) Thornhill Press

Veevers, G. Pocket Guide to Aquarium Fishes (1980) Mitchell Beazley

Ward, Dr. A. Questions and Answers: The Tropical Aquarium (2007) Intepret Press

Whitehead, P. How Fishes Live (1975) Elsevier Phaidon

Magazines and Periodicals

Aquarium Fish (USA)
Practical Fishkeeping (UK)
Tropical Fish (UK)
Tropical Fish Hobbyist (USA)
Tropical World (UK)

Websites

www.aquahobby.com
www.aqaulink.com
www.aquariumhobbyist.com
www.fishkeeping.co.uk
www.fishgeeks.com
www.londonaqaurium.co.uk
www.thetropicaltank.co.uk
www.tropicalfishkeeping.com

The author and publishers would like to thank everyone who allowed us to borrow, use and photograph fish, equipment and settings.